Around the World in 80 Cruise Ships: Out East and Down Under

Julia Verne

Table of Contents

Introduction..1
PART I: North America and East Asia.........7
Queen Mary 2..8
Crossing the continent by train..............................19
The *Amsterdam*..40
JAPAN: Hakodate..55
Tokyo...62
Kyoto..71
Nagasaki..77
PART II: South Korea to Indonesia............83
SOUTH KOREA: Jeju City, Jeju Island.................85
CHINA: Beijing...93
Shanghai...109
Hong Kong..113
VIETNAM: Nha Trang..121
Ho Chi Minh City (Saigon)......................................128
SINGAPORE...135
INDONESIA..145
Semarang, Java...146
Komodo Island...154
PART III: Australasia and home...............163
AUSTRALIA..165
Darwin...178
Great Barrier Reef and Brisbane.............................182
Sydney (and beyond)..186
NEW ZEALAND...211
South Island...214
North Island...219
Crossing the Pacific by cargo boat.........................235
JAMAICA: Kingston..249
Queen Mary 2 (again)..253

Introduction

'Good morning, ladies and gentlemen, this is your Captain. For your information, the unusual vibrations we experienced earlier were caused by an earthquake. A tsunami warning has not been issued, and there is no cause for alarm. We will update you as soon as we know more. Meanwhile, please relax and enjoy the rest of your day aboard our beautiful ship.'

An earthquake at sea? Not really something we were expecting, even though this Pacific crossing had already been somewhat unsettling.

A couple of days out from Seattle, the ship had changed course to avoid a heavy storm. We were all in favour of this more northerly route because if anything went wrong we would not be far from the chain of Aleutian Islands that stretch from Alaska almost to Russia. Gale force winds still caused pitching and rolling, and many gave dinner a miss the next night; perhaps more serious for some – if not us – that evening's song and dance show was cancelled.

Then Wednesday disappeared. Admittedly, this was not unexpected as we had crossed the International Date Line some time during the night, meaning we went to bed on Tuesday and woke up on Thursday. But things got even stranger: the bridge and mahjong players nearly came to blows in the card room and security had to be called, while at dinner I was presented with a cake and six waiters gathered round to sing me an enthusiastic Happy Birthday. Only it wasn't my birthday.

Then came the earthquake. We were beginning to wonder if we had done the right thing booking the cruise. The omens were not great, but obviously there was no turning back. We took comfort in the fact that, short of fire or norovirus breaking out, we would soon reach the safety of our first port, Kushiro in Japan.

Next day:

'Good afternoon, ladies and gentlemen, this is your Captain. We have reports of a typhoon sweeping up through Japan and predictions of 60-knot winds, which means, unfortunately, that I have decided to cancel our first port of call, Kushiro. We are liaising with the Japanese authorities to arrange an alternative port.'

What were we doing in the middle of the Pacific, and where were we going? But first, allow me to introduce my wife, Mrs Verne:

- **Yes, Mrs Verne here**, author of the internationally acclaimed first volume in this *Around the World in 80 Cruise Ships* series. I am kindly letting my husband, Mr Verne, write some of Book Two as it keeps him occupied and out of trouble. However, I have reserved the right to comment whenever I feel like it, and to chip in with something entertaining whenever he starts weighing you down with too many facts – as I've often told him, just because it's true doesn't make it interesting. Or when he shows bad judgment. I mean, he wanted to call this book *20,000 Leagues Across the Sea*, claiming that we did actually travel an equivalent distance. I had to point out that people might confuse it with a book of similar title by Jules Verne, or think we were deliberately using his name for our own advantage. Ridiculous.

Back to Mr Verne then. For the moment.

After we retired early from our office jobs a couple of years before and returned from what we then thought was our trip of a lifetime – to the Caribbean and around South America – we had settled into a comfortable, rather humdrum life in the English town where we had worked for thirty years. (Yes, we're English, which explains the spelling and punctuation.) But then the travel bug started to bite. We had never been to East Asia, and Mrs Verne had long wanted to return to the land where she had spent the first seven years of her life – Australia. On that earlier trip we had jumped from one cruise ship to another because of cowardly Mrs Verne's fear of flying (rivetingly described in *Around the World in 80 Cruise Ships: How We Cruise Hopped the Globe Without Ever Setting Foot in an Airport* (the first in this gripping series, if you haven't yet bought it). Could we no-fly cruise again, but on a much larger scale?

After some research we found that we could indeed hook up a series of cruises to take us around the Pacific Rim and back – five ships in all, stopping at 26 ports sandwiched between 60 or so days at sea, and a number of weeks ashore in the US, Australia, New Zealand, and US again. Say, 6 months in total. Once we'd lined them up, we booked the first four ships all in one day, seven months in advance. Luckily, we were able to secure permission from the New Zealand and US immigration authorities to disembark in the middle of two of the legs (getting off mid-cruise always proves expensive because the company insists on charging the full amount, which we accept as an inevitable side effect of our little cruise-hopping habit).

This is how it looked:

> Southampton, UK to New York (*Queen Mary 2*, Cunard)

> Seattle to Sydney, via Japan, South Korea, China, Vietnam, Singapore and Indonesia (*Amsterdam*, Holland America)

> Sydney to Auckland, New Zealand (*Celebrity Solstice*, Celebrity)

> Tauranga, New Zealand to Savannah, USA (*Matisse* cargo ship, CMA CGM)

Like Christopher Columbus, we would head west to discover the east.

We resorted to a cargo boat simply because we were unable to find a cruise for New Zealand to the US, but to our surprise this no-frills mode of transport cost about the same as a cruise. Anyway, we thought, at least it would make an interesting change. Mrs Verne had in fact been on a cargo ship in the 1990s when our jobs took us to the States, spending two weeks crossing the Atlantic with our two young sons (that fear of flying again), while I flew across well in advance. My excuse, naturally, was that I could make the necessary arrangements – renting a house, buying a car, checking out schools – in readiness for their arrival. My contribution was extremely valuable, of course, although Mrs Verne muttered that I didn't have to chase a five-year-old round a rusty hulk back in the days before Health and Safety was invented.

Now, with no children to worry about, we rather looked forward to the adventure of crossing an even wider ocean in a freighter instead of a cruise ship.

Then we discovered that the US visa waiver programme doesn't include cargo vessels. We had to take a trip to the US embassy in London for an interview and pay hundreds of pounds for B1/B2 visas permitting entry at Savannah from a freighter. On the other hand, these visas would allow us up to six months at a time in the States rather than the three granted under the waiver system, and were valid for the next ten years. In our eyes we now became travellers with special status, and unlike your average tourists passing quickly through we would be free to roam America at our leisure. Mrs Verne had her doubts, though:

> • **Yes,** I would just like to point out a little hiccup in Mr Verne's planning here. Roaming the US like buffalo would very much depend on having a rental income from our house in England, as by then we would have run out of money – and as yet there was no sign of a tenant. That meant we couldn't book the final leg home to the UK because we didn't know how much time we would be able to afford in the land of the free. I have no idea why I agreed to this.

6

PART I: North America and East Asia

Queen Mary 2

From personal experience, staggering round a transatlantic liner in a dinner jacket with a martini is the normal, rational, <u>reasonable</u> way to cross the Atlantic. Heading for an airport and strapping yourself to a flimsy aluminium tube is an unfortunate and eccentric aberration.

(Mark Smith, The Man in Seat Sixty-One travel website)

Say, when does this place get to New York?

(actress Beatrice Lillie, on boarding the enormous *Queen Mary* in the 1930s)

In late August, after weeks of getting the house and garden ready for a tenant that still hadn't materialised, we drove down to Southampton on the south coast and spent the night at my brother's. After dropping the car off next morning at a long-term storage place we checked in at the cruise terminal, then it was up the covered ramp to be scanned aboard *Queen Mary 2*, greeted by smiling staff in their smart red tunics, gold buttons and pristine white gloves. With a quick look at the amazing six-deck-high Grand Lobby atrium (we'd seen it before – as described in the first in this series, go on, buy it – and we'd be seeing it plenty more), we headed for our cabin. From being dropped off at the terminal to finding our 'stateroom' had taken just twenty minutes.

As we headed into the Solent later that afternoon the ship turned not in the westerly direction you might expect, but east, in order to follow the deep water channels around the Isle of Wight. This circuitous start to the journey had its attractions: portside was Portsmouth's soaring modern Spinnaker Tower, glinting in the fading light, and also a rare close-up of a 19th-century sea fort, while to starboard were surprisingly clear views of individual houses on a very rural-looking Isle of Wight. Even Fawley Oil Refinery's smoking chimneys seemed romantic when silhouetted against the setting sun behind us.

By the time *QM2* rounded the island and turned west, it was already dark and we were back in the cabin, relaxing before dinner. Rather than an inside cabin without natural light or fresh sea air, a budget option we sometimes take, this time we had chosen one with a 'sheltered' balcony. For 'sheltered' read 'solid steel': it sheltered us perfectly from any views of the sea. Yes, you could enjoy the sea breezes and admire the view while standing, but if you sat down you faced a wall of metal, like sitting in a tin can. Not a big problem, just a little odd if you are used to glass-fronted balconies (even odder, Cunard's website doesn't show the balcony at all and there is no explanation of what 'sheltered' means).

The explanation is that for the three decks below the Promenade deck, balconies are cut right into the hull, because *QM2* was designed to plough through rough Atlantic seas and this requires more steel than on standard cruise ships. Sheltered balconies are cheaper than the conventional ones on higher decks and, to be fair, do offer protection from the elements, though you are still at the mercy of the chain smoker next door. (Smoking on balconies is banned, of course. In theory.)

The crossing on this occasion – and most transatlantic crossings, in our experience – was pretty smooth. We frequently sat out, and had no complaints about the stateroom itself, which was comfortable, well appointed and with enough space under the beds for our mountain of luggage.

Our four dinner companions were English: a retired couple and a young couple who were moving to Boston. We quickly slipped into the role of old hands who had lived stateside for several years and had plenty of advice to offer (whether they wanted it or not). The 8:30 sitting was a bit late in the evening for us but at least allowed extra time to digest afternoon tea, of which more later.

The restaurant we had been assigned to, the Britannia, was spectacular: a vast space on two levels under a beautiful Tiffany-style glass ceiling, hosting up to 1,200 diners at a sitting. Our waiters were impressively efficient, though we were not always so impressed by the food, and portions seemed meagre. We soon adopted what was a common practice in the Britannia of ordering more than one starter and/or dessert. At least the plates were hot – cold plates in restaurants are a pet peeve of ours, much to the amusement of friends and family back home, who seem happy to eat lukewarm meals. (Both our sons have rebelled against their eccentric parents by insisting on eating off nothing but icy-cold plates). You'd think the sheer size of the Britannia would make it difficult to keep food hot all the way from the galley to the more distant tables, but the plates are loaded at 100 degrees onto special trolleys and – fortunately for the waiters – served with a heat-proof cloth.

QM2's menus are tailored to suit whichever region the ship may be visiting – lighter dishes for the Mediterranean, heavier for colder northern climates – and the mix of nationalities on board at any time may also have an influence. One Cunard head chef has observed, for example, that American passengers like their beef as filet mignon, while the British prefer beef Wellington (we do love our pies). Lower down the food chain, nationality will again determine the proportion of steak pie versus burger sales in the more casual dining areas.

We returned to the Britannia restaurant a couple of times for lunch, when you are assigned a table by the maitre d' and it's pot luck who you will be sitting next to. On this trip, with 800 Germans on board out of 2,400 passengers, it was not surprising that on one occasion we shared a table with a group from Germany. They spoke very good English, and conversation was easy. Something at the back of our minds made us slightly nervous, however: in the TV sitcom *Fawlty Towers* the advice that hotel owner Basil Fawlty (John Cleese) gave to his staff before they served some German guests was 'Don't mention the war!', which became a popular catchphrase in the UK. Would we now blurt out something embarrassing to our lunch companions? We needn't have worried, as literally within five minutes the *Germans* started talking about the bombing of Coventry. We managed to agree that the way we had destroyed each other's cities was regrettable and that war was terrible (although they started the whole thing), and moved on to a more comfortable subject – the lunch menu, perhaps, or whether anyone was going to that evening's Abba Night.

(On this crossing, the few announcements made over the public address system were in both English and German. Each message took a while, but not a problem. Imagine being on a cruise with Italian company MSC, which makes announcements in *five* languages.)

One problem with the Britannia – or not, depending on your point of view – is that a quick lunch there is impossible. You may be casually dressed, but the trappings and service are still formal and unhurried, and anyway you are happily absorbed in getting to know your interesting new acquaintances. An hour and a half flies by. But make a habit of this and you are on a downward spiral. At your first lunch, you swap stories about families, jobs, and home life, but most of all about previous cruises and places visited (as they say, travel broadens the mind but lengthens the conversation). You have a glass or two of wine and eventually leave feeling nice and mellow. Next day you lunch with more new tablemates, who ask the same questions of you as the day before, and ditto you of them. This time you leave with head gently throbbing. And, annoyingly, you realise after a day or two that you've no appetite for all those delicious scones and cakes at teatime. Then it's time for dinner ('Oh God, already?'). To bed, exhausted. Finally you opt for modest buffet lunches for the rest of the voyage, avoiding all conversation with strangers. Or is that just us?

The scale of the Britannia restaurant is matched by the approach from the lobby, where large bronze bas-relief murals are displayed on either side, each depicting a region of the world. Icons featured in the North America panel include a baseball player, the space shuttle, a Native American, and the Statue of Liberty, but there, barely visible, is something so subtle you might not notice it unless told where to look: a tiny Homer Simpson watching TV from his sofa. He's tiny because the artist chose not to mention it to Cunard.

The evening menus in the Britannia can get a little samey and unadventurous. If chicken consommé, vegetable ravioli and treacle pudding with custard are not exciting enough for you, there's the Verandah restaurant at the stern of the ship, but this has a cover charge. A typical three courses might be frogs legs sucette or poached quail eggs, followed by lobster tail and octopus carpaccio or Australian grass-fed Wagyu beef, and to finish, chocolate ganache and delicate tonka bean mousse with speculoos biscuit and olive oil ice cream. We only know that from reading the menus outside. Never went, obviously. Too mean.

As mentioned in the celebrated *Around the World in 80 Cruise Ships: How We Cruise Hopped the Globe Without Ever Setting Foot in an Airport*, passengers in suites have privileged access to one of two Grill restaurants, much smaller and quieter than the often-noisy Britannia. No set mealtimes here: guests can come and go at their leisure, even breaking off mid-meal and returning later for dessert and coffee. 'Savour the ultimate in dining sophistication', says Cunard, which translates to à la carte menus, more emphasis on presentation, and space for dishes such as steaks or crêpes Suzette to be prepared at your table. The Queens Grill encourages guests to order off menu, with reasonable notice. According to QM2's head chef:

We don't have everything on board. Sea frog, kangaroo, antelope whatever – we need to order it before the guest actually arrives. So, we need enough notice to order it from shoreside. But anything that is on board, there is no question asked, we always accommodate their requests.

A useful tip – always order your antelope steak in advance.

We did take some exercise to offset all the eating – a token effort, really, considering that a brisk 30-minute walk burns around 150 calories, equivalent to, say, a third of a large blueberry muffin. Mrs V usually woke up early and headed out to a mostly deserted Promenade deck for a few laps and some bracing sea air. I was more intent on securing my full English breakfast at the buffet, though I did manage to walk a mile or two between afternoon tea and the evening meal. On inclement days I exercised indoors by striding along the stateroom-only corridors. *QM2* being such a huge ship, its endless, empty corridors can spook you, and I half expected to turn a corner and suddenly see those twin girls from *The Shining*, horrific blood-soaked apparitions beckoning to me ('Hello, Mr Verne. Come and play with us, for ever... and ever... and ever.').

Incidentally, if you walk the shorter circuit up on deck 12 you will see the ship's kennel quarters, affectionately known as the poop deck. A New York fire hydrant and a vintage lamppost from Liverpool were recently installed to make the dogs feel at home. A week in the kennels could set the owner back by up to $1,000, but that does include freshly baked treats, exercise, room service and professional photographs. Next time we're going as dogs.

There was more to our life on board than food – just. That week's activities included a talk 'By Royal Appointment' about the Queen's art collection, the Royal Ascot Ball, and workshops by Royal Academy of Dramatic Arts graduates. Spot the theme? But there were also all the usual cruise activities such as flower arranging, bridge, ballroom dancing classes, trivia quizzes, and scarf tying (why is that a thing?), and more demanding pastimes included watercolour classes, choir rehearsals, or fencing lessons. Plus, of course, the many social groups: LGBT, solo travellers, needleworkers and knitters, book clubs, masonic brethren, military veterans, 'Friends of Bill W' (a euphemism for AA meetings), Christian Fellowship and, last but not least, Welsh speakers. There was no excuse for doing nothing, although of course that's what we mostly did.

Cunard also has an exceptional lecture programme, often featuring celebrity speakers. The rumour is that true A-listers tend not to get hired because they always want the best suite for themselves and perks for their entourage. But lesser known experts in their field are surely more interesting: Concorde test pilot, war-zone journalist, espionage specialist, astronomer, prison governor, and so on. For further enlightenment there are daily shows in the planetarium, and this week not just any old opera screening in the cinema, but an opera in 3D.

QM2 passengers certainly have high expectations for the quality of service on board, and for the most part they are satisfied. Some people will always try to take advantage of any mishap, however: in 2018 a woman from the UK said she was making a 'massive complaint' and demanded £3,000 compensation (out of the £9,000 she'd spent on the trip) after the ship suffered a complete power outage that lasted all of fifteen minutes. Scots singer Midge Ure was on the same crossing, updating his many Twitter followers regularly but failing even to mention the incident, which may not have helped her case.

Finally, after a week at sea, we arrived in New York, the sun shining brightly on fine views of the Statue of Liberty and the new World Trade Center. We disembarked at the Brooklyn Cruise Terminal, picked up the rental car, and left the city via the Verrazzano-Narrows Bridge that *QM2* had only narrowly squeaked under just hours earlier. (Shortly before the toll booth there's a road sign that reads 'Leaving Brooklyn? Fuhgeddaboudit'. On another bridge the sign says

'Leaving Brooklyn? Oy Vey!'.) Within a few short hours we had arrived in Baltimore to stay with our son and his family for a week before setting out to cross an entire continent – by train – from sea to shining sea, with a detour up into Canada, then boarding the Holland America ship *Amsterdam* in Seattle towards the end of September.

> • **Mrs Verne again:** We enlivened the hot and humid week in Baltimore with a trip to Baltimore Harbour and Fort McHenry, where US troops repelled the British in 1812 (the nerve). Our final day was in the Annapolis area where we used to live when working in the US, to renew contact with the best BBQ emporium of all time, Red Hot & Blue. We needed to fortify ourselves for our upcoming train ride, where there would be no opportunity to wash or change clothes for over 24 hours...

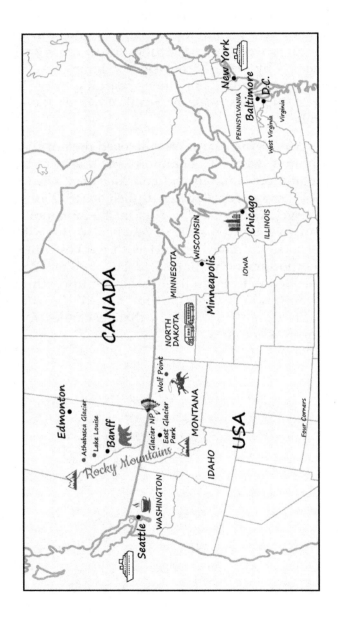

Crossing the Continent by train

'And you like it here?'

'In America? Oh, yeah! It's good. It is so big! So green! So wide – wide – wide!'

(Jonathan Raban, *Hunting Mister Heartbreak*)

You might think a description of a long train ride out of place in a book about cruises, but trains are just like cruises on land – stuck in a small place with the same crowd of people, subject to whatever food is on board, and longing for stops to break up the occasional monotony. Of course it's also <u>not</u> like a cruise: no onboard entertainment, for instance, and no sea, though I suppose the prairies we were about to pass through did look like a sea of grass. But we had to cross the continent to get to the next ship and we weren't going to fly. Apologies to US readers for telling them much they will already know, but a great deal was new to us and yes – we were truly excited about travelling by Amtrak…

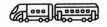

Days 1–2

We boarded Amtrak's *Capitol Limited* train at Washington DC, heading for Chicago. Our bags had been checked until Minneapolis, as if we were at an airport – why can't British trains adopt the same system for long-haul journeys, instead of forcing passengers to struggle with cases and fight to find space in crowded carriages? Amtrak even sells cardboard boxes to take the overspill from your luggage if it turns out to be overweight – something we were glad of when the souvenirs started mounting up.

Soon after departure, a woman in a nearby seat complained loudly that the FBI had set her up by seating her next to a Mexican man (she disappeared later, removed from the train by security personnel). Within an hour we were trundling slowly across the historic bridge at Harpers Ferry, where two rivers and three states meet in a dramatic setting. Thomas Jefferson called it 'perhaps one of the most stupendous scenes in Nature… This scene is worth a voyage across the Atlantic.' You could only agree. Harpers Ferry had been the scene of the doomed attempt in 1859 by abolitionist John Brown to start a slave rebellion. He failed, but the resulting song ('John Brown's body lies a-mouldering in the grave/But his soul goes marching on' etc.) became a favourite with Union troops in the Civil War.

The train continued on through the backwoods of West Virginia, to the frequent accompaniment of its mournful whistle (imitated in song by Hank Williams as 'that low-wa-wone-some whistle'). Wifi aboard was non-existent. The only networks my phone detected were in towns as we passed through, and top of the list at one point was 'FBI Surveillance Van' (were they onto us?). Meals were available in the dining car – not great – while the little café sold mostly junk food but was useful for coffee or tea. The first time I ordered hot tea in the café the attendant added two sachets of honey on the side, which I gave back, thinking this was very odd but not saying so. He was pretty surprised too. Next morning he recognised me: 'No honey, right?'.

Although with Amtrak there's more space than on UK trains and you can tip the seat right back until you're *almost* comfortable, we had stupidly forgotten to pack any warm clothes or blankets, and so shivered all night in the air conditioning. We barely slept. Luckily we were spared the agony of listening any more to the most boring woman in the world, who somewhere behind us had spent all evening talking loudly about herself to some unfortunate person next to her before mercifully falling asleep.

Next morning, Chicago, where we emerged blinking and dishevelled, having slept in our clothes but at least cleaned our teeth on the train. We had until 2pm before boarding the *Empire Builder* to head out west – still in the same clothes, of course. A shower was still a long way off so we should have avoided anything strenuous in the heat and humidity, but instead we went for a long sweaty walk to see huge Lake Michigan, enjoying the occasional breeze and shade as we passed through the skyscraper canyons (the word 'skyscraper' was coined right here, and you can see why).

Over the next few days, the flyover states – so called because, as the old joke goes, nobody ever alights there – would be passing slowly outside our train window. Chicago to Seattle would have been 46 hours straight, but we had decided to break the journey by alternating a night on the train with one in a hotel to recover. We'd booked coach seats all the way. Sleepers ('roomettes') are expensive – hundreds of dollars on a long journey – and we never sleep well in them, although the privacy and limited extra space are welcome. Amtrak does have an unusual option that may save you money: a few days before you leave, it invites you to upgrade your coach seat by entering an online auction. You only hear if you have been successful on the eve of departure. We did this on a recent cross-country trip, and my cheeky bid of $295 was accepted for a roomette advertised at well over $500.

Our first night's break was at Minneapolis, Minnesota, which we reached later that evening. Along the way, Wisconsin was a lot of flat, green countryside, pleasant though a little dull, but then suddenly on the Wisconsin/Minnesota border we crossed the mighty Mississippi. A bit of a surprise to see it that far north.

Day 3

We slept like logs in the Minneapolis Days Inn after our night of horror on the *Capitol Limited*. A notice on the door of our hotel room advised 'In case of tornado, call Front Desk', but even a tornado would not have woken us. Refreshed, we hit the streets but found them strangely empty. On entering a shiny modern building in search of coffee, we discovered where everyone was: many buildings downtown are connected by a network of glassed-in walkways allowing pedestrians to avoid the rigours of winter and summer out on the streets. They really do say 'Oh yaaa' round here, and it's infectious. Didn't hear 'you betcha', though. After a lazy lunch of Reuben sandwich for me – salt beef, sauerkraut and melted swiss cheese between grilled rye bread – flatbread pizza for Mrs V and beer for both of us, our worthy plan for visiting the Institute of Arts crumbled. We decided to go to the famous Mall of America instead, taking the light rail Hiawatha Line via Minnehaha station (no, I did not make this up). It may be one of the largest malls in the world, but the shops were far less interesting to me than the full-size indoor roller coasters and giant Lego models. A sign at the entrance read 'The Mall of America bans guns in these premises', but luckily we'd left ours in the hotel.

Late that evening we boarded another *Empire Builder*, but not before enduring the tedium of Amtrak's antiquated seat allocation system, which typically goes like this. You can't reserve a seat in advance, so at least half an hour before the train is due, and without any prompting, a queue mysteriously begins to grow in front of an empty desk. The train may well be running late, but the people in the line just stay there; they have travelled on Amtrak before and know the score. Boredom is now and then relieved by the antics of some little kid or an eccentric local who has wandered in, to be shooed off by a kindly official: 'Now, now, Mary, you know you shouldn't be in here pestering folks. Off you go.' Finally, as the train arrives a uniformed conductor appears at the desk and asks the same two questions to each in turn: 'Where ya goin'?' and 'How many?'. He shuffles various bits of paper working out what seats are still free, scribbles your seat numbers on another piece and hands it over. This repeats until the queue is no more. We have never figured out the advantage of being towards the front of the line, as all seats appear to be equal and everyone with a ticket gets a seat. Someone should tell Amtrak about computers.

Now finally on the train, we could see that two backpackers were being held by police on the platform, having been ejected from the train for drunkenness. Amtrak certainly doesn't tolerate bad behaviour, even if the word 'timetable' means nothing to them. In *Around the World in 80 Days*, as Phileas Fogg was about to take the train from San Francisco to New York, his servant Passepartout recommended buying a few dozen rifles to defend against any attacks by the Sioux and Pawnees. Having now seen paranoid and inebriated persons removed from our trains, we sensed that the biggest danger we faced might be our fellow passengers.

Again, very little sleep overnight.

> • **Mrs Verne here:** We had warmer things with us by now, but it was difficult to get entirely comfortable, although some people seemed able to sleep like logs. They do turn the main lights out at about ten and all announcements cease, but people are constantly moving around to step outside at the stations for a smoke, when time allows, or to go downstairs to the bathrooms. It is at this point that all comparisons to cruising come to a grinding halt with an agonized squeal of brakes. As in all trains on all continents, the bathrooms are necessarily tiny cubicles, and I'm sorry to disclose that after some usage on a very busy train they bear no comparison to the gleaming, constantly buffed up palaces of cleanliness on cruise ships. Let's just say that you have

no choice but to keep using them, not only for the usual purpose but also to clean your teeth and occasionally drag a comb across your bedraggled head. Actual washing is impossible because of the cramped conditions and the constant flow of passengers needing their turn. People all want to get ready for the night or freshen up in the morning at about the same point, so you try and time your visits to avoid the worst rush but inevitably get someone rattling at the door just as you unzip your wash bag. Then the train jolts sideways, your toothbrush drops onto the ghastly floor, and you have to throw it away and clean your teeth with your finger.

Day 4

A long day lay ahead – however furred up and unfragrant we were feeling – with the vast American plains of North Dakota undulating past, studded with small lakes and low hills in soft Tuscan colours. And pretty much empty. Back in the 1990s when we criss-crossed the mid-West in an RV camper van with our two young sons, I would research ahead of time to pick out some wacky attraction that might relieve the boredom of long days on the road. I have fond memories – if not the rest of the family – of stopping at Four Corners, where you can stand with your feet simultaneously in Colorado, Utah, Arizona, and New Mexico, and of rolling into a place in Iowa that claimed to be the future birthplace of *Star Trek's* Captain James T. Kirk. Our eldest son, teetering on the edge of adolescence, often refused even to get out of the vehicle, but he *was* quite impressed by Captain Kirk's birthplace.

With our passage by train through Wisconsin and North Dakota, I was one step away from achieving something that few Americans manage, or perhaps even want to do: visiting all fifty states. I had now chalked up forty-nine – all except Hawaii. (Granted, our experience of some states had been rather brief, like that half-hour in a Nebraska supermarket just over the state line, or the time it took to drive the forty miles across Rhode Island.) A visit to Hawaii would not be easy, though, because of Mrs V's silly little no-fly rule. The only way we'd ever get there together would be on a luxurious 14-day round-trip cruise from California (well, if we must...).

Meanwhile, around midday on day 4 the *Empire Builder* arrived at Wolf Point, Montana, complete with howling wolf sculpture on the platform, a reminder that wolves had been hunted here in frontier times. The town, on a large Native American reservation, is home to the Wild Horse Stampede and the Montana Cowboy Hall of Fame. We were definitely in the American West now. The only other feature to appear out there in the wilderness were the nodding donkeys of oil wells – just one or two here and there, presumably giving local farmers extra income as a result of the fracking boom at the time.

Origins of some place names seen so far (for the factually interested):

Minnehaha: Lakota word meaning 'tumbling water'

Winona: Sioux for 'firstborn daughter'

Mississippi: Ojibwe for 'big river'

These long-distance trains were massive, double-decker beasts, with most of the seating and sleeping areas on the upper deck. In the middle was the observation car, a long, glass-domed lounge area that offered wonderful views of the passing scenery but attracted a mix of the odd and the gregarious (some people there were both; we were neither). On our trip it was also a favourite hangout for the many Amish families on board, who played endless card games with much laughter and chat in their own language.

On we rolled for hours and hours. At rare intervals, the conductor would announce that a 'smoke and stretch' break was coming up, giving passengers a few minutes on the platform before the familiar 'All aboard!' call (as with cruise ships, the train will not wait for you). Strangely, most people stayed put, while hardcore smokers were first off and the occasional fit-looking person would ostentatiously power walk up and down. We just ambled, glad of the fresh air and a chance to stretch our legs. The monotony of the journey was only otherwise broken by drinks in the café or a meal in the formal dining car. We had brought a coolbag of food along for something better than we could get in the café, but as time passed the contents became less and less appetizing, to the point where the café's microwaved pizzas with their list of 85 ingredients began to look pretty darn tasty.

By the way, Montana is the 48th most densely populated state in the USA. In every square mile of land, there is an average of just seven people. England has an average of 1,119 per square mile. Sorry about the stats, but it's what Bill Bryson does and he sells millions.

Late that evening, still in Montana, the train arrived at our next stopover point – East Glacier Park, gateway to the Rockies (separated by a common language, the British say *glassier*, Americans *glaysher*). We were about to zip up into Canada to see an old schoolfriend of Mrs

Verne's, then zip back down again to pick up the same train and finally hit the coast.

Days 5–8

To the park lodge next morning, the lobby a huge open space with a high timbered roof supported by rows of 30-foot tree trunks, from which glassy-eyed buffalo and moose heads looked down upon us as we drank espressos in comfortable old armchairs. Having picked up our rental car from the local general store, we drove north through the Blackfeet Indian Reservation. Our first task was to find somewhere still in Montana for a picnic lunch, because if we left it too long we risked having it confiscated by hungry Canadian border guards using food import regulations as an excuse. We didn't manage to find a lunch spot sufficiently far away from a bear trail for my ease of mind but in the event, the kindly, semi-retired customs officer with a love of hiking and a cabin in the nearby woods had no interest in our cheese and crackers. We hoped that US immigration would be equally nice and friendly on our return.

Next day, the novelty (for us) of a drive-thru Starbucks:

Me: Two small Americanos, please.

Girl at window: Tall Americanos?

Me: No, small.

Girl: Tall is small.

After a look at lovely Banff in its mountain setting (where a diner waitress was very surprised when we said we wanted to finish the soup before she brought the main course – those crazy Brits and their liking for hot food) we took a winding road up into the national park and soon had a classic encounter with a bear. Seeing people gathered by the side of the road watching something, we peered through the trees and, sure enough, there was a bear on the railway tracks, busily scrabbling in the dirt. We edged nervously forward for a better view.

An approaching train whistled repeatedly and the bear stood on its hind legs as if to confront it. Some tense moments followed as we all willed the bear to chicken out, followed by utter relief as it backed down and hopped off the tracks. But relief turned to panic as it started to run *in our direction.* I swivelled and almost knocked Mrs V over (**Mrs Verne:** I can confirm this) but we made it to the car. After the train had passed, the bear ambled back and resumed its digging. We later learned that it was a grizzly (dish-shaped face, hump, long claws) – a rare sighting, locals told us – and that it was probably trying to get at grain dropped by freight cars.

The Canadian Rockies were incredible, highlights for us being the beautiful but cold Lake Louise and its magnificent lodge where the bell hops were in Tyrolean lederhosen, gorgeous Pyramid Lake, stunning Peyto Lake with its vivid turquoise waters and contrasting deep green conifers, and the awe-inspiring, slowly retreating Athabasca Glacier.

Pyramid Lake

Before leaving the park in late afternoon, we stopped to relax a little at a hot springs where you could hang about in the gloriously warm water gazing at the mountain scenery, and then choose a nutritious snack from the array of health foods on offer: pies, cakes, and cappuccino. We had the lot.

Days 9–13

During our stay with Mrs V's dear old friend near Edmonton in Alberta, we and all our luggage took over her basement for two nights, spent a day seeing the sights with her, and on the last evening were joined by her lively brood of adult offspring for a wonderfully boozy meal out. Basically we were treated like royalty – but then they get very few visitors in Canada, and those snowy winters can be so very long.

On our way back south to pick up the train again something far more horrific occurred than our near-death experience with the bear. After a night in the neat, well scrubbed little town of Cardston in Alberta we went out in the morning for coffee – and couldn't get any. I should explain, for those who have inexplicably failed to read our first book, that coffee is very important to us. Things turn pretty ugly if we don't get it (well, Mrs Verne does, anyway). The lady in the bakery explained that there were many Latter-Day Saints living in Cardston, and they didn't drink tea or coffee – too sinfully stimulating. (Yes, that's why we like it. Mormons don't drink alcohol either, so just as well we weren't staying another night.)

We crossed the US border with ease, but without the friendliness shown by that nice cuddly Canadian border guard earlier. At last we could go for a sinful coffee, screeching up to the first café over the border to order an Americano the way we like it – double espresso, half the water.

An article in the local Montana paper caught my eye with a proposal that executions should be halted – because they were too expensive. When we went back outside, our rental car's Missouri licence plates were attracting interest:

Hi, where in Missouri are you folks from?

Ah, no, we're from the UK, actually. It's a rental car.

Oh. Saw your licence tags. Thought you were from Missouri. Pity, never met anyone from Missouri.

Now I could achieve something I'd been denied back in the 1990s – a visit to Glacier National Park in Montana ('The Most Beautiful 50 Miles in the World'). In the past, after being driven thousands of miles in an RV around the natural wonders of America, the family had put their foot down when a small detour to this park was suggested, insisting on going the short way across Montana instead, although obviously there is nothing 'short' about that state. And so, on this hot, sunny day many years later I finally got to drive the winding Going-To-The-Sun Road, past a sparkling blue lake and up as far as the giddying heights of the Continental Divide. We picnicked by that lake, cautiously, near a sign warning us there was no guarantee of our safety in bear country.

These picnics became a regular feature as we went on. It was the sensible solution for a quick, cheap lunch anywhere we chose, and we took any opportunity to stock up on salad, cheese, crackers and fruit, so that at the drop of a hat we could stop and eat quickly, enjoying the view, and then move on.

During our RV trip all those years ago we had crossed Montana in the opposite direction, though in our dash to get home we barely deviated from the interstate, only stopping at the Little Big Horn battlefield site, and once for drinks at a place so small that the election posters simply said 'Jim for Sheriff'. 'Beautifully desolate. Big sky, rolling road, rocky hills, lush green grass, yellow wildflowers, huge clouds banked up,' I wrote in my diary at the time, clearly impressed by these landscapes. Author John Steinbeck was too. In his *Travels with Charley: In Search of America*, his classic account of a road trip around America with his French poodle in 1960, he wrote that he was 'in love with Montana. For other states I have admiration, respect, recognition, even some affection, but with Montana it is love, and it's difficult to analyze love when you're in it.'

The trouble is, journalist Bill Steigerwald did some checking in 2010 and concluded that the book was more fiction than nonfiction, and indeed later editions even acknowledge that Steinbeck took liberties with the facts. Like us, he had barely strayed from the main highway in Montana, so according to Steigerwald 'his love affair with the Treasure State was more like a two-night stand'. The local paper for East Glacier, writing about these revelations, repeated the famous lines above but added drily: 'Imagine what he would have written if he would have spent a week here.'

Well, whatever the truth was, we've been there and I think Steinbeck was right: you truly can fall in love with Montana after only a couple of days travelling across it. And we didn't take any liberties with *our* facts.

It was time to get back on the *Empire Builder* for the final stretch to Seattle.

- **Mrs Verne:** So, on the train again – the stunning scenery but also the long hours, the terrible food, the nights tossing and turning in our coach seats trying to get comfortable, and the dread of visiting the bathrooms. Our whining was in stark contrast to the stoic attitude of the usual groups of Amish passengers, who certainly seemed to be frequent and enthusiastic train travellers. Well known for their spurning of modern appliances and simple, generally farming lifestyle, the Amish were fascinating to observe. All were dressed alike, the men in braces, wide-brimmed hats and shirts mostly of the same one or two plain dark colours, the women in long, plain dresses of the same sorts of tones with their hair neatly tucked into little white caps. The groups we saw always seemed to be travelling as families, older grandparents and young couples, often very young themselves, but already with one, two or even three babies and toddlers in their arms. The children were all quiet and well behaved except for the very tiny babies, and when they cried or fussed the young husbands – all bearded like the older men, and sporting pudding-basin haircuts – would take their turn carrying the little ones around or taking them to the café for a change of scenery.

On this train the adolescents or young couples still without offspring congregated in a section of the café to play cards and chat in Pennsylvania Dutch – not Dutch at all, but a variety of German imported by the first settlers in the eighteenth and nineteenth centuries. I could remember some schoolgirl German, but had trouble making any sense of what we occasionally overheard. It would have been interesting to talk to one of them, and I kept smiling in a friendly way at some of the women with babies, but they seemed reserved and happy in their own company. Their patience with the long delays and poor conditions – changing babies in those bathrooms must have been a nightmare – put me to shame.

After the usual nightmarish night we reached Seattle in the morning. Late again, although we counted ourselves lucky that none of the four trains had been delayed more than an hour or so. Amtrak is notorious for its delays, understandably so, perhaps, because it covers such huge distances, but even the Trans-Siberian Railway manages to be punctual. Delays are mainly due to slowing down and even stopping, multiple times, for higher-priority freight trains to go through. Everyone is resigned to this fact, and no one takes the train unless their plans are flexible. We've suffered some extraordinary delays on Amtrak since. One train we took from San Francisco to Grand Junction, Colorado, arrived 12 hours late, at 10:30 at night – a whole day lost. This was no surprise to the café attendant, who had predicted at breakfast time that we would still be on the train for dinner in the evening, and we were. If only we'd hopped onto a freight train like a couple of hobos we could have reached our destination hours earlier.

But, can you believe, Amtrak does not pay any compensation for delays. Conversely, and this is just as surprising if you think about it, in the UK a 'delay repay' scheme refunds the ticket price *in full* for a delay greater than sixty minutes. You often get an ironic cheer in the carriage as the clock ticks past the hour. British trains are not very reliable either, so it's a wonder that they make any profit. We know people who manage to travel just about free by judicious use of the lines more prone to delay.

Days 14–16

What do you do on arriving in Seattle? Order espressos, of course, and they were perfect. (We briefly contemplated moving here permanently when Mrs V noticed there was an espresso stand every ten feet throughout the city.) Second priority was checking in at our B&B in the Capitol Hill district. We asked the Ethiopian cabbie what the area was like, and he said 'gays and lesbians', to which we had no reply.

During our three days in the city we had meals al fresco as cosmopolitan Seattleites strolled by: office workers, tourists, panhandlers, the interestingly dressed, and the oddly behaved. It was lively, yet relaxed. In Pioneer Square the official 'busker of the day', a violinist, entertained the lunch crowd while on the periphery a few individuals – possibly homeless – kept to themselves. It was enjoyably egalitarian: we could never be sure whether that scruffy eccentric with the heavy carrier bags was a vagrant or a software billionaire on his way back from the shops.

Seattle's waterfront indoor market was a vast, century-old emporium housing traders of all kinds, 'where the fish and crabs and shrimps lay beautifully on white beds of shaved ice and where the washed and shining vegetables were arranged in pictures' (Steinbeck came here too – or said he did). The fish stalls were stacked high with fresh Alaskan halibut cheeks, jumbo lobster tails, foot-wide Dungeness crabs, baskets of Fanny Bay oysters, live crawfish, plump wild king salmon, Columbia River sturgeon steaks, golden trout, fresh monkfish, banks of cooked peeled shrimp, and fancy king crab sections from the cold clear waters of Alaska. Tables in the market's seafood restaurants looked out onto amazing Puget Sound.

As well as predictable sightseeing around Seattle, we took a short ferry ride back in time to Vashon Island, charming and old-fashioned, with a few farms, winding country roads and one small town. This lush, unspoiled rural idyll is also a haven for artists, writers and outdoorsy types (or hippies, as some on the mainland call them). There is certainly an alternative-lifestyle-and-local-community vibe along the town's main street: Saturday farmer's market, organic café, 'Expresso and sustainability advocate' (but not an advocate for the correct spelling of espresso, apparently), Save the Plankton fundraising campaign, and poster for the Tallest Weed and Biggest Zucchini contest, plus antique shop, bookstore, art galleries and tea shop.

Betty MacDonald, the comic writer who shot to fame with her bestselling memoir *The Egg and I*, lived on Vashon in the 1940s and wrote about it lovingly, though with some wry comments on the weather:

The climate, about ten degrees warmer and wetter than Seattle and vicinity is ideal for primroses, currants, rhododendrons, strawberries, mildew and people with dry skin who like to read. The population is around five thousand people and an uncounted number of snivelling cowards who move back to the city for the winter.

Vashon hosts an annual Strawberry Festival, which is odd because the island's strawberry farms died off in the 1980s, and few berries are for sale at the festival, but the locals still celebrate the memory. This year's festival had been a classic of small-town Americana, we heard: we were disappointed (and I'm not being sarcastic) to have missed the shopping cart drill team, kazoo marching band, classic car parade, and maybe a concert by local band Poultry In Motion.

On our final morning we packed and headed for the cruise terminal, feeling very excited. Since leaving Southampton it had taken us a whole month just to get to here, which was really the starting point for our voyage to East Asia. (Not 'the Far East', my sensitivity reader tells me, as that's Eurocentric. As an Australian Prime Minister once pointed out: 'What Great Britain calls the Far East is to us the near north.') Having enjoyed the comfortable familiarity of North America and awakened memories of previous times, we were now looking forward to new experiences. Japan, South Korea, China, Vietnam, Singapore, and Indonesia lay ahead.

The *Amsterdam*

I must go down to the seas again, to the vagrant gypsy life,
To the gull's way and the whale's way where the wind's like
a whetted knife;
And all I ask is a merry yarn from a laughing fellow-rover,
And quiet sleep and a sweet dream when the long trick's
over.

(John Masefield, *Sea Fever*)

So far in our various travels Holland America had been our favourite cruise line. Would this next mammoth cruise of fifty nights and 14,000 miles live up to expectations? We had a couple of nagging doubts, given that the Pacific was very wide and would take ten days to cross:

1. What if the ship had a technical problem?

2. Worse, what if our dinner companions were not fellow-rovers with merry yarns?

Late morning check-in for the *Amsterdam* was seamless, and again we were in our cabin within twenty minutes and lunching soon after. At the sailaway party, a large 'Welcome Home' banner didn't need explaining to the many returning faithful: Holland America cruisers are a very loyal lot who sail again and again. The Lido Deck was bright with strings of colourful naval flags, but visibility out in Puget Sound was characteristically poor as ferry boats emerged eerily from banks of fog and nearby islands remained wreathed in mist. With little to see and dampness in the air, we took advantage of free rum punch before exploring the ship's interior.

The *Amsterdam* was a medium-sized ship, less than half the tonnage and passenger capacity (around 1,300) of *Queen Mary 2*. At this stage there were only about 800 passengers on our Grand Asia and Australia Voyage, giving us all some welcome extra space to relax in, and 600 crew members to attend to our needs.

Being a relatively old ship, built before balconies became almost de rigueur on the more modern megaships, only a quarter of its staterooms could boast one. At least we had an outside cabin with a picture window for a decent sea view and plenty of daylight, having deliberately avoided any of the cabins looking out onto a deck for the obvious reason that passers-by could look in. The cabin itself was not what you might call spacious. The 'lounge area', as Holland America optimistically called it, was a narrow space leading from the bed to the bathroom. Yes, it was physically possible to lounge on the sofa, set your drink down on the tea-tray-sized table, stretch your legs until they touched the desk on the opposite wall, and raise your head at an awkward 45 degrees to watch the TV fixed up by the ceiling. For relief from this unnatural pose you might lower your head, only to see yourself a few feet away reflected in a huge wall mirror. The most comfortable position for watching TV proved to be lying on the bed, which was lovely until you fell asleep halfway through the programme. Divining the reality behind cruise line hype before parting with your cash is not a new problem:

State-rooms on ocean liners are curious things. When you see them on the chart in the passenger-office, with the gentlemanly clerk drawing rings round them in pencil, they seem so vast that you get the impression that, after stowing away all your trunks, you will have room left over to do a bit of entertaining—possibly an informal dance or something. When you go on board, you find that the place has shrunk to the dimensions of an undersized cupboard in which it would be impossible to swing a cat.

(PG Wodehouse, *The Girl On The Boat*)

Our en-suite was roomy enough and the shower had shampoo and conditioner dispensers fixed to the tiles like bottles of spirits in a bar (if only), while the hair-dryer unit next to the sink was industrial strength 'salon quality'. Bathrobes – nay, 'deluxe waffle weave and terry cloth bathrobes' – were supplied 'for use during your voyage', an unsubtle reminder not to filch them at the end of the cruise. One small and pleasing detail that other ships seldom have was a thick curtain between the 'lounge area' and the cabin door, meaning we didn't need to block light around the door at night with bathrobes and coats as was our usual custom. Before booking the cabin we had done our research, but found that most cruisers posting on, say, cruisecritic.co.uk, seemed to be suite people who talked about their spacious balconies, freebie wine and chocolates, special meals, exclusive lounge, binoculars, and so on and so on. I know all this is available if you pay enough, but where were the Cruise Critic members writing about the more modest accommodations? In the event we found our Holland America stateroom to be generally comfortable, in a good location, and of a size expected for the price we had paid.

We were happy to have been assigned to the later dinner sitting, starting at 8pm. However, our first evening meal did not go well, leaving us feeling somewhat deflated. Our three companions were an older English lady, sweet but also rather deaf and possibly senile, Frank, a pleasant elderly American man in a similar condition, and his wife, younger, glammer and more with it. Yet she was the bigger problem: voluble, a bit manic, and not interested in anything we said, even when we were answering her questions. Despite resembling Imelda Marcos she made me think of Marilyn Monroe in *Gentlemen Prefer Blondes*, when at the first mealtime on board ship she fires questions at her table companions without waiting for their replies:

Marilyn to 1st man: Are you enjoying your trip?

1st man: Well...

Marilyn to 2nd man: How many times have you crossed?

2nd man: This is my third...

Marilyn to 3rd man: Don't you feel alone out on the big ocean?

3rd man: Well I uh...

Marilyn to all: I just adore conversation, don't you?

But where Marilyn's character was bubbly and good-natured, this lady was self-centred and domineering. She talked at length, left few gaps, and made clear her opinions and what our opinions should be too. Maybe we were being a little harsh on her, given that she came from a different culture and English was not her first language. Or maybe not. Either way, we had a problem.

The first full day of a cruise is great for freebies. On the *Amsterdam*, as well as a free glass or two at a welcome aboard lunch, wine was the favourite inducement at the art gallery and the shops, while free jewellery, free bingo tickets and a complimentary tour of the spa were on offer too. Once you take the bait, of course, you're on an 'exclusive' invitation list for all future events. It is also the day for the Cruise Critic 'roll call' group to have their first Meet and Greet. For the last year or so, anyone booked on this cruise would have been able to log on to the Cruise Critic website and get in touch with fellow passengers, asking questions or arranging onshore excursions together with local tour guides. Such independent outings are competition for the ship's own tours, and yet Holland America (HAL for short) actually provides the space and free refreshments for Meet and Greets, where more than a hundred people often turn up. A HAL rep even comes along to offer support and express appreciation for everyone's loyalty and, later in our cruise, this group was presented with commemorative printed menus at a special lunch in the dining room. All very generous of the company, maybe, but it's clearly good business sense too, and indeed some other cruise lines also foster relationships with their Cruise Critic groups.

Companies hand out freebies and look after us well; we feel the love and buy stuff from them. That's an open and honest transaction. The problem I have is when journalists and bloggers write clichéd puff pieces in exchange for free cruises, restaurant upgrades and interviews with the captain. Why should you trust their opinions? More to the point, why is no one offering *us* a complimentary cruise? I can only assume that Holland America and Cunard haven't yet read *Around the World in 80 Cruise Ships: How We Cruise Hopped the Globe Without Ever Setting Foot in an Airport*, where we said some *very* nice things about them.

A couple of days in came the big storm that opened this book, and the Captain's evasive action. As the rocking and rolling continued next morning I wanted to do a Groucho Marx, calling the engine room in *Monkey Business* pretending to be the captain: 'Oh engineer, will you stop the boat from rocking, I'm gonna have lunch.'

And then, in mid-Pacific, was when Wednesday disappeared. Yes, we had crossed the International Date Line during the night, meaning we went to bed on Tuesday 12 hours behind GMT and woke up on Thursday morning 12 hours ahead. Or, as Mark Twain summed it up in *Following the Equator*,

While we were crossing the 180th meridian it was Sunday in the stern of the ship where my family were, and Tuesday in the bow where I was.

Strange disturbances on board – like that dust-up among the players in the card room and the very public celebration of my birthday that wasn't – were unsettling when our brains were already confused about what day it was, so we were definitely not prepared for what followed. Promenading on deck during a period of relatively calm seas we felt a sudden judder run through the ship, as if we'd hit a rumble strip mid-ocean. Puzzled looks all round as the *Amsterdam* ploughed on. After some delay the Captain made his announcement about the earthquake, its epicentre a volcano a few miles north of us. It was the first time he had experienced an earthquake at sea, he told us (not reassuringly).

Having endured an interesting week at sea so far, with barely any land in sight other than a few barren-looking little islands on the horizon, we just wanted to make it safely to our first port of call, Kushiro in Japan, but then came news of the typhoon and the decision to cancel Kushiro. We would re-route through the Russian Kuril Islands, past the tip of Sakhalin, and down the west coast of Japan rather than the more exposed east coast where Kushiro was. Landfall would now be Hakodate, at the bottom of Hokkaido, the large island in the north. We didn't care where it was; any port in a storm and all that. As compensation, complimentary wine appeared at dinner, making it a lot jollier than usual.

Yes, jolly, because to our shame, back on the fourth day we had asked the maitre d' to find us another table in the restaurant, leaving our difficult dinner companions behind. We're still ashamed (and never did it again) but it was going to be a long, long voyage and we didn't want to spend the whole time being bellowed at. The night after the move we were the first to arrive at our new table for six, which was in a great location on the upper level next to a large window, and we waited with some trepidation to see who would be joining us. Two couples approached, hesitant and a bit puzzled. They had, after all, spent the last few evenings together and were not expecting anyone else at their table, but once we explained the situation they were very welcoming. Both couples were Australian, Paul and Karen in their fifties, Doug and Maureen in their early seventies, and it was immediately obvious that they were livelier and far more fun to talk to than our original table. Australians and Brits largely share a sense of humour and have a lot of popular culture in common, although Australians are probably more familiar with British TV than the reverse (apart from *Neighbours*, of course). Our new friends saw the joke later in the cruise when we pretended to have abandoned them in their turn for the affable Canadians on the neighbouring table, and indulged us whenever we played our little game of arriving early to dinner and sitting separately and not in the usual places. Seat swapping to sit next to a different person keeps the conversation fresh. (Etiquette experts say that separation of married couples at table avoids public displays of affection putting fellow guests off their food, and they also advise putting intellectuals opposite each other in order to spark debate. Not relevant to us on either count.) **(Mrs Verne here:** How dare you?)

One afternoon, a few days after meeting our new Aussie friends, we came across Frank, the frail old man we'd originally been seated with, leaning on a walking frame by an elevator and looking bewildered. To our surprise he recognised us and said he was lost and needed help finding his stateroom, so of course I took his arm and we slowly guided him back home. He was so grateful and made absolutely no reference to our disappearance from the table (luckily, his wife wasn't around). We felt pretty guilty when leaving Frank as he waved us off and urged us to go and enjoy ourselves.

I may not be able to get ashore tomorrow to see Pompeii. There's some talk of holding the final of the deck-billiards.

(*Punch* magazine cartoon)

Crossing the Pacific would take us ten days in all, eight of them 25 hours long. (If you are ever uncertain as to what day it is, HAL can help. All the elevators have rugs with the current day spelled out in large letters for the confused.) We were able to fill all those days and hours without too much effort – literally. We joined a trivia quiz team, which became an enjoyable daily event. We read a lot, napped, did research in the well-stocked library, wrote up our diary, went to the cinema and attended worthy lectures on globalisation, oceanography, photography and upcoming ports. HAL talks are usually enlightening, though the speakers can be a little dry. For variety, I also joined a few outdoor sporty events, at one of which the games host remarked how much I looked like Rod Stewart. Blond, spiky-haired Rod would have to be wearing a rather more kempt black wig to even remotely resemble me, but still, I took it as a compliment (possibly). People always seem to think I'm someone on the entertainment side – on various other ships I've been taken for a musician, a lecturer, and a ventriloquist, so this time it was flattering to be likened to an ageing rocker love-god. I think.

Once upon a time, long, long ago (the 1950s), games on board ship were simple and straightforward – mostly quoits, shuffleboard, table tennis, and this kind of thing:

There is a variety entertainment in the saloon which they call 'Sex-A-Pool'... The men and women are made to blow up balloons and then to sit upon them as a test of courage. They are then required to hang clothes on two washing lines, to give farm yard imitations, and to eat spaghetti blindfold... Then the games-instructor and the swimming-instructor take off their clothes, put on female bikinis, don comic hats, and do an imitation of American chorus girls singing whoopee songs. It is excellently done and they are almost of professional standard.

(Harold Nicolson, *Journey to Java*)

Innocent times. Fast forward to the 2020s:

ROBOTRON is a state-of-the-art robotic arm with an attached gondola that seats three guests. The adrenaline-pumping experience gives riders an unobstructed view of the horizon as they hang over the edge of the deck, flip upside down and move in all directions... Positioned in front of a giant video screen, the ride will then bounce and twist in time to music visualised as colourful patterns and pulses of light.

(Press release for MSC *Seascape*)

Call me old-fashioned but that sounds like absolute hell. I enjoy a bit of ping-pong or paddle tennis, though shuffleboard is too sedate ('a deck game that involves pushing little round slices of wood all over the place while waiting for the next meal to happen', according to Lawrence Lariar's *Nautical Dictionary*). Competitive ping-pong doubles were an almost daily event on the *Amsterdam*. Although the other players were usually older than me, they meant business and I had to have my wits about me, remembering to jump out of the way as soon as I'd played a shot to allow my partner to leap forward to face the return. The rules for who served in what sequence and when you changed ends were beyond me, so I left it to the professionals. I did lose once in singles to a young woman, but there were perfectly valid reasons for it: to paraphrase satirist James Thurber, the table was too short and the net too high, the bats were warped, the ship rocked and I had something in my eye.

The traditional games at sea provide at least *some* exercise, whereas fun on modern megaships is becoming more and more sedentary. On the latest MSC ships you can enjoy 3D cinema with boneshaking seats and a wind machine, or go full virtual reality by donning headsets to fight zombies or fly a jet plane. Some Norwegian Cruise Line ships have a real, physical go-kart track, the most extreme one snaking over three decks. But here's the catch: the more sophisticated fun of today comes at quite a price. Most activities are not free, and of course these being family ships there is great pressure on parents to cough up. 'Nickel-and-dimed' is a phrase seen in quite a few online reviews.

It's not just the big family-friendly ships that have gone digital. Even cruise lines with a more mature clientele now seem to assume that everyone has a smartphone. They will boast about their 'integrated digital ecosystem' or similar and will encourage you to download their app, which incidentally does work on the ship's free wifi, so an internet package is not needed to use it.

Unless you're a technophobe – and spare a thought for them: being told on a ship to put your phone in airplane mode must be confusing – some aspects of this digital revolution are certainly welcome. Use the app to read the daily programme, or book a table, excursion or spa appointment. The app will remind you before an event starts, and will open a map to show where it's on and even where you are at the moment (also useful for finding your cabin). You can sign up for the 'chat' feature to message other guests, but there may be a fee. And some apps include a kid locator service via a digital wristband, which might also work for tracking your spouse to the bar, where he's enjoying the novelty of a robot bartender so much that you may have to go and drag him away.

However, cruise ship apps are not always as seamless as the cruise lines claim, dependent as they are on a good wifi network and user-friendly software. 'Unreliable and difficult to use' is a typical online verdict, with the suggestion that the cruise lines should hire some 14-year-olds. Of course, the result of having a digital ecosystem will be that everyone carries their phone or tablet around and stares at the screen. Just like at home.

We counted the days as we slowly and uncertainly – or so it seemed – made our way towards Japan. Why does anyone go on a long cruise? I would guess, in ten words or less, that most would answer something like 'get away from it all, meet new people, enjoy myself.' And visit other parts of the world, of course, though for many this is a secondary consideration, and indeed industry experts like to say that the ship itself is the main destination of a cruise vacation (not for us). In simpler times than ours, one could just head off over the horizon and leave any worries behind. The sea takes trouble away, says Henry James in *The Patagonia*:

...takes away letters and telegrams and newspapers and visits and duties and efforts, all the complications, all the superfluities and superstitions that we have stuffed into our terrene life.

Well, yes, but not if you buy an internet package. Want to meet new people? You are obviously more sociable than professional cynic Clive James, who sailed from Australia to England in 1962 and after weeks at sea came up with this bleak assessment in his *Unreliable Memoirs*:

Even a luxury liner is really just a bad play surrounded by water. It is a means of inducing hatred for your fellow men by trapping you in a confined space with too few of them to provide variety and too many to allow solitude.

'Hatred' may be overstating it a tad. As for enjoyment, while planning your trip you note all the on-board activities and the interesting itinerary, and you take it for granted that you will have a good time. There are bound to be imperfections due to factors beyond your control – a small problem in your cabin, food not hot enough, a disappointing excursion – and you tolerate them. But you are overlooking one important thing in all this: yourself. Philosopher Alain de Botton in *The Art of Travel* describes his first morning on holiday at a Barbados hotel: dawn light, beach, coconut trees, lapping water, birds in flight. Idyllic. Yet on later reflection he realises that he had not been fully attentive to the scene, and with dry humour he reveals a startling explanation:

I may have noticed a few birds careering through the air in matinal excitement, but my awareness of them was weakened by a number of other, incongruous and unrelated elements, among these, a sore throat that I had developed during the flight, a worry at not having informed a colleague that I would be away, a pressure across both temples and a rising need to visit the bathroom. A momentous but until then overlooked fact was making its first appearance: that I had inadvertently brought myself with me to the island.

JAPAN: Hakodate

Early October. Finally, we sailed into Hakodate harbour in warm sunshine and docked some way out of town, next to a scrapyard. Before passengers were allowed to disembark we all gathered on an outer deck and watched as, on the quayside, a team of ancient Japanese men unfurled a banner of welcome, dignitaries in black suits stood to attention and schoolgirls in sailor suit uniforms lined up behind. Miss Hakodate, immaculately dressed in a plain cream dress, high heels, lace gloves and her sash of office, stood by. The welcome banner also advertised a snack called surume – a kind of chewy shredded squid – with the slogan 'the more you bite it, the better it tastes'. Our Captain made a speech in return and was given a brightly coloured tunic with a red squid cartoon character on the back.

After this impressive welcome, passports were inspected on board and our horde of rather more casually dressed Westerners could go ashore. From the shuttle bus into town we saw signs warning people to be careful of tsunami, a reminder that in 2011 Japan's largest ever earthquake off its east coast created a tsunami which killed thousands and caused a meltdown at the Fukushima nuclear plant. Luckily, the population of Hakodate had time to evacuate before the tsunami hit, and damage was mostly to buildings. These signs and the earthquake at sea that the *Amsterdam* had experienced a few days earlier brought home to us that our itinerary was taking us along parts of the Ring of Fire, a not-quite circle of volcanic activity around the Pacific. We would see more dramatic evidence when we visited New Zealand later on.

The harbour area was spick and span. Knowing no Japanese, we frequently hadn't a clue what the small waterfront businesses were just from their shopfronts, and even when we went in and checked out their products we were often none the wiser, as many items were neatly wrapped in cloth or coloured paper. We found a self-service coffee machine but as all labelling was in Japanese we pushed buttons at random until the right colour liquid emerged. Surprisingly good espresso. The nearby fish market was no mystery, if unlike any we had ever seen before: giant crabs being weighed on scales, legs waving in the air; silvery sprats preserved and packed in cellophane, rows of eyes staring out at you; and banks of other unidentifiable denizens of the deep, although a bilingual sign did at least try to help: 'This fish is fishy'. One stall offered a fresh squid delivery service, mailing you a live specimen in a capsule (returns not accepted). And you could buy squid ink ice cream. But the most popular part of the market, judging by the crowd of locals and fellow cruisers milling around, was the catch-your-own-squid tank. Here, you dangled a mini fishing rod over the tank where scores of the little creatures were going round and round, and as soon as you caught one a lady quickly gutted it and handed it back to you on a plate, totally raw and still flapping. We didn't linger.

The squid tank did not completely spoil our appetites, though the lunch we eventually opted for was not a great success. Further along the waterfront we decided to try a restaurant based on nothing more than its modern, clean appearance. Inside was a large board showing three prices in the middle of much Japanese script, and a greeter in smart uniform.

Mrs V: Hello, do you speak English?

Greeter: (bows, shakes head)

Mrs V: Well, can you tell us what these are? (points to items on board)

Me: He doesn't speak English.

Mrs V: I know, but I'm pointing.

Me: But we won't understand his reply.

Greeter: (smiles, says something in Japanese)

Mrs V: I don't understand what he's saying.

Greeter: (smiles, repeats)

Mrs V: Sounds like 'biking goo'.

Me: Ah yes, that means a buffet.

Mrs V: What? Since when do you know any Japanese?

Me: It's actually 'baikingu', from our word 'Viking'. You know, as in smorgasbord. I read about it in the guidebook.

Mrs V: Oh, of course, I should have guessed. That's what the Vikings were famous for, wasn't it? Rape, pillage, and buffet lunches.

Me: (I smile at greeter, point to lowest price, nod) We'll take that one, please.

The greeter ushered us politely to a sink at the side, making it pretty clear that he would not let us through the turnstile he was guarding until we had washed our filthy Western hands. The buffet itself was baffling – we barely recognised anything on offer so picked items at random, not knowing whether to use a bowl or plate, whether the dark liquid was soup or sauce, or which items were savoury or sweet. Mrs V was uncertain what to make of it all and ate little, whereas I, more diplomatic or just more adventurous, filled my plate and ate heartily.

Time to explore. We climbed up into the Motomachi district overlooking the harbour. Hakodate was one of the first Japanese ports to open up to Western trade in the 19th century, albeit after a bit of gunboat diplomacy from US Navy Commander Matthew Perry, whose statue stands in a local park. The architecture here reflects those foreign influences, including the colonial pile that is the former British consulate, a Russian Orthodox church and a Catholic church. We wandered Motomachi's charming old streets, a marked contrast to the soulless modernity below.

Back down at sea level, the Museum of the Northern Peoples had interesting exhibits on the indigenous Ainu tribe, who had roamed much of the country until successive governments turfed them off their lands and suppressed their culture, to the extent that today there are only about 25,000 Ainu left. British explorer and writer Isabella Bird spent several weeks here in the late 1800s and clearly became very fond of her hosts:

...they are attractive, and in some ways fascinating, and I hope I shall never forget the music of their low, sweet voices... The savage look produced by the masses of hair and beard, and the thick eyebrows, is mitigated by the softness in the dreamy brown eyes, and is altogether obliterated by the exceeding sweetness of the smile...

And we could see from the museum's artefacts – clothing made from tree fibres, embroidery, wood carvings – that despite primitive living conditions Ainu culture had been highly sophisticated.

Many years ago, when I was in my thirties, we hosted two Japanese girls in the summer while they attended an English language school. On the day that hosts and students met each other for the first time, several girls at the event seemed to be showing a strange and unexpected interest in me. It turned out that I bore a striking resemblance to a famous Japanese actor. So, on this our first visit to Japan I was braced for excited females requesting selfies, but... nothing. My public had forgotten me. Mrs V then pointed out that I was a retired English civil servant, and not actually a Japanese actor. As we waited later for the shuttle bus to take us back to the ship, some groups of giggling schoolgirls were in fact hanging around, but they were flirting with the young Indonesian crew members waiting near us.

Nevertheless, there are consolations to being a tourist of a certain age, as American writer Paul Theroux noted: 'Being invisible – the usual condition of the older traveller – is much more useful than being obvious. You see more, you are not interrupted, you are ignored.'

On our departure we were treated to another ceremony by our Hakodate hosts, but this one was informal and way more fun. As the ship slid away from the dock, scores of children lined up on the quayside to wave us off, the younger ones in bright yellow or green jackets and matching bandannas, older schoolgirls in smart uniforms, all hopping, clapping, stepping left then right, and marching on the spot (we later found it was the squid dance, which everyone here learns as children and performs at festivals.) They kept it up until we could no longer see them.

Already it was becoming obvious that we weren't in Kansas (or Gloucestershire) any more.

Tokyo

The port city of Yokohama is gateway to huge, teeming Tokyo. No welcome ceremony on this occasion, so we brave independent travellers disembarked without delay and shared a taxi to the station, where buying tickets was not a problem. Our train was standing room only at this hour, shared with solemn, silent commuters identically dressed in dark trousers and white shirt and carrying a briefcase (known as 'salarymen'). Once in Tokyo, thirty minutes of urban sprawl later, we walked to the nearby Imperial Palace Gardens, an oasis of calm amid the surrounding bustle of traffic-heavy roads. The gardens were more like a European municipal park and not very Japanese, apart from some massive stone walls and wooden guardhouses, and the actual palace – a 1960s replacement for the original that was destroyed by bombing in 1945 – was off limits. It was hot and very quickly we began to wilt. Venturing into the much cooler subway, we found that colour coding of the lines at least made interpretation of its spaghetti-like network a little easier. Buying tickets from a machine was also simple, and if you happened to underpay, a fare adjustment readout at the end of your journey told you how much you owed.

Lunchtime. On port days, regulations forbade taking food off the ship for a picnic lunch. So, we scoured a department store in the upmarket Ginza area for a) food that we recognised, and b) a place where we could eat it, like a food court or just a bench in a park. The entire basement was devoted to a vast array of foods, but nothing was suitable as a takeaway lunch and we could see nowhere to sit anyway. However, up on the top floor were a few restaurants and after some hesitation we plumped for a small place with only six tables and two waitresses but also, crucially, a menu partly in English. Green tea and hot towels came first, then our orders of noodle broth were brought on wooden trays with unidentifiable vegetables on the side. Broth may not have been the wisest choice. After a few minutes of fumbling with my chopsticks I had soup stains down my shirt, and the attentive waitress came over, bowing and apologetic, to give us spoons and paper bibs. We didn't enjoy the food too much, but that was our own fault, and at least we had tried something new.

Outside again, a young woman saw us puzzling over our map and kindly helped us work out the subway route to Asakusa, a district known for temples and traditional crafts. Unlike Hakodate, where they were probably sick of swarming cruisers, in Tokyo (and later in Kyoto) someone – always female – appeared at our sides and offered to help if we seemed at a loss. Although it was the opposite of what you might expect of a city, part of the explanation could be that more English speakers are to be found there than in the provinces.

At the heart of Asakusa is Tokyo's spiritual epicentre: the city's largest and oldest Buddhist temple, Senso-ji, and its five-storey pagoda. But to reach the temple complex we first had to work our way along a narrow street heaving with mainly Asian tourists, all shuffling along as slowly as possible to gawk at the scores of little stands selling tacky souvenirs and street food. Then, as we finally broke free and approached the temple we passed between two lines of brightly lit paper lanterns decorated with bold Japanese script – not wisdom of the ages, we learned later, but adverts for local businesses.

Senso-ji Temple was founded in the 7th century but has been rebuilt several times due to earthquake, fire and war. The current edition dates from 1958. Before entering the temple people stopped at a large metal cauldron belching pungent smoke from incense sticks, and fanned smoke over themselves in the belief that it could cure an ill. Most seemed not to take the ritual too seriously, yet presumably felt it might work.

Another ritual was taking place just inside the temple: fortune telling. In front of a long bank of wooden drawers was a little metal box with a hole in the bottom. According to the instructions posted above, you 'shake the box politely a few times', a stick slides out of the hole with a number on it, you find the drawer matching that number and take out a slip of paper telling you your fortune, in Japanese, English, and Chinese. The instructions also included some excellent advice:

When you draw good fortune, you should not be careless and arrogant. Even if bad fortune, have no fear. Try to be modest and gentle. Whether in good or bad fortune, you should tenaciously do your best. You can carve out your own fortune.

Nearby was a kiosk selling lucky charms labelled 'good marriage', 'lucky with money', 'don't worry', 'safe childbirth', and best of all: 'wishes come true'.

A Shinto shrine stood next to the temple. Shinto has no doctrine, sacred text or regular services, but it does have gods and spirits – literally millions of them. Rituals and festivals are very important. Typically, a worshipper will first wash their hands in the purification fountain outside, then drop a coin in the collection box, ring a bell to greet the resident spirit, clap hands twice, bow, say a prayer, bow again and retreat backwards. As with Buddhist temples you may try your luck at a fortune, and annul any predicted misfortune by twisting the paper onto tree branches, which we were to see at several shrines in Japan.

Shinto and Buddhism coexist in Japan in an unusual way. Surprisingly, perhaps, the Japanese mix and match the two religions and view them as complementary. It is common practice to pray at Buddhist temples and Shinto shrines (often located in the same grounds), and to have two shrines at home. And while the vast majority of Japanese weddings take place in a Shinto or Christian ceremony, most funerals are conducted with Buddhist rites.

One 400-year-old festival that we were sorry to miss at Senso-ji was the sumo crying baby contest, held every April. In this 'competition', two sumo wrestlers stand in a ring, each holding a baby. At the referee's signal, the sumo do their best to make their baby cry first, by jiggling the infant up and down and making funny faces, but then if these tactics fail they bring out the scary demon masks. If both babies begin bawling at the same time (pretty likely, I imagine), the one who cries loudest and longest is the winner. Fifty or so babies are allowed to take part each year, and there is much demand for places because the parents believe that crying babies grow to be strong and that the festival drives away evil spirits.

We couldn't leave without experiencing another side of Tokyo life – Shinjuku, the entertainment district. It was very busy, full of young people, neon lights, 24-hour shopping, possibly some red-light activity but we weren't sure, and nowhere obvious for us to eat (again). We went briefly into a pachinko gambling parlour just to have a look, and it was as noisy as an engine room, stinking of cigarette smoke and full of people glued to row after row of what looked like vertical pinball machines. I took a couple of photos, but this attracted the attention of a Yakuza gangster type who glared at us so menacingly that we fled the scene. After soaking up some more local colour we resorted to a non-fishy Italian meal and a welcome beer inside a shopping arcade, then returned by train to the ship, exhausted.

Japanese people had seemed very formal in the city and in the metro, but of course were far more relaxed in the red light district – where our visit was strictly observational, of course.

Everything in Japan so far, from the language barrier to the inevitable culture clash, had seemed alien to us. But *we* were the aliens – clumsy, clueless giants who dribbled food, couldn't work a simple vending machine and needed help with maps.

There is a danger nowadays that with the availability of such wonderful online resources as Tripadvisor, travel blogs and Google Street View, you get sucked into researching the heck out of every location until going there no longer seems quite worth it. But isn't it better to leave some things to the imagination, then enjoy it when your hazy preconceptions meet reality or you suddenly learn something completely new and unexpected?

Veteran travel writer Dervla Murphy made a similar point, seeing a generation gap in attitudes:

In the travellers' world, social media have enlarged the generation gap. The internet has brought a change in the very concept of travel as a process taking one away from the familiar into the unknown. Now the familiar is not left behind and the unknown has become familiar before one leaves home. Unpredictability – to my generation, the salt that gave travelling its savour – seems unnecessary if not downright irritating to many of the young.

(Foreword to *To Oldly Go: Tales of Intrepid Travel by the Over-60s*)

She is right about the influence of the internet, but some members of the older generation appear to have succumbed too: witness all those questions on Cruise Critic from more mature cruisers wanting to know exact details of the where and the what and the how before they venture anywhere. And that includes me, somewhat: for a recent non-cruise holiday I found myself studying satellite photos like a CIA analyst in order to check out Airbnb properties, and scrolling through reviews of launderettes. We do all seem to be losing the thrill of the unknown, which author William Least-Heat Moon called 'the addiction of the traveler', and replacing it with something safer and more predictable. Incidentally, Murphy, who specialised in going to inhospitable, far-flung places by bicycle or mule before old age forced her to retire, once said that she'd pay £10,000 not to set foot on a cruise ship as it would be her worst nightmare. Well, *my* worst nightmare would be getting attacked by wolves, robbed at gunpoint or bitten by a scorpion, all of which she suffered on her many travels.

Although I do like to be prepared to some extent, on this trip around the Pacific there were more destinations than I had time to read about in advance, and you can't use a ship's slow, expensive internet service to spend hours doing research. Instead, we resorted to photographing pages from modern guidebooks in the *Amsterdam*'s library. Older guidebooks are of less practical use but still have entertainment value. *Murray's Handbook for Travellers in Japan* (1907) mentions in passing that in Tokyo 'the rite of Walking Over Fire may be witnessed at the temple of Ontake on the 9th and 17th September. The less interesting Ordeal by Boiling Water takes place on the previous day.'

Next day, with the *Amsterdam* due to set sail at noon, we stayed in Yokohama and toured its Silk Museum, which had good exhibits about sericulture (silk farming, which I didn't know even if you did), displays of kimonos, and live silkworms eating mulberry leaves. By cranking the handle on a mechanical model we were able to tease threads from several cocoons onto a plastic rotating bottle. Unbelievably, it takes 9,000 cocoons (pictured below) to create one top-quality kimono.

As usual, I splashed out on a couple of bookmarks for my extensive collection back home. (Did I mention that I collect bookmarks from around the world? I keep them in a box file and bring them out to show friends and family whenever I can, which makes me very popular.) Both were of ladies in kimonos – one painted delicately on wood, the other an origami figure glued onto cardboard – and each, in true Japanese style, was a miniature masterpiece.

After Hakodate we were expecting another official send-off, but the Yokohama authorities did not oblige. An ad hoc gathering of locals on the landscaped roof of the cruise terminal did wave to us as we set off, though. As we sailed away the *Amsterdam* began serving 'Kamikaze' cocktails to the passengers on deck, and in the evening the TV movie was *Paradise Road*, a drama about Japanese atrocities in World War II.

> • **Mrs Verne here.** I thought this grossly insensitive, as some Japanese passengers had just boarded. I went to complain to the entertainments officer, who grudgingly apologised.

More serious echoes of war were to crop up at various points along our route, and within a few days things were going to get a whole lot darker.

Kyoto

fading temple bell
the scent of blossom strikes me
in the evening

(Haiku by the poet Basho)

At our next port of call we were greeted by a 'Welcome to Kobe' banner, firefighter band, mascot, Miss Kobe, police chief, and assorted flag wavers. Now that was more like it. These people had made an effort. The brass band was smart in cream uniforms and gold-braided caps, Miss Kobe looked most regal in a formal pastel blue dress with matching hat and white gloves, and the nautical-themed mascot bounced about enthusiastically.

Buoyed by this welcoming party, we went on our independent way with Aussie friends Paul and Karen from our dinner table. Not tempted by the ship's own tours – a day in Kyoto plus bullet train was $US 250 per person – we took the free shuttle bus to town, then taxi to the bullet train for the ancient city of Kyoto, fifty miles away (about $50 each, but only $10 when we returned later on the regular, slower train).

Bullet trains depart and arrive on time, their seats are comfortable, the ride is smooth – at up to 200 miles per hour, so fast it's uncomfortable looking out of the windows – mobile phone users are discreet, public announcements are minimal, and the conductor bows every time he enters or leaves the carriage.

All unheard of in the UK, so for the next twenty-eight minutes we were wide-eyed out-of-towners. These trains have been in service in Japan since the 1960s and form a national network. By contrast, the USA has had a few high-speed sections in the north-east only since 2001, while the UK's short stretch of high-speed track south of London has been operational only from 2007. Before then, Paris to London was like riding a rocket until you emerged from the Channel Tunnel, and then it was clown car the rest of the way to the metropolis.

In the next day and a half we wandered the streets of Kyoto and explored at length. A castle, a garden, and a temple were the highlights of our visit.

Nijo Castle was the residence of a 17th-century shogun, and with its moats, massive walls and watchtowers it looked the part. At the centre of the castle was an opulent palace, full of beautifully painted screens, decorated ceilings and delicate carvings. The wooden floors had been cleverly designed to sound like nightingales when stepped on, so that an intruder would be unaware that his presence had been detected. We padded along, shoeless as per Japanese custom, and the sounds made by the floorboards were exactly like the songbirds we later heard in the gardens.

Afterwards we hesitantly entered a small pavilion in the grounds for a tea ceremony, sitting cross-legged on a tatami mat while green tea and a pink sweet were brought by kimono'd ladies. We had no idea what the proper etiquette was, but the ladies were evidently well used to gauche tourists and we were able to relax and enjoy the view over the landscaped gardens. The British had been here before. Prince Charles and 'Diana-san' came to Kyoto in 1986 for a quick-fire round of visits to temples, gardens and their own tea ceremony in the grounds of this very castle.

Shosei-en Gardens were a tranquil haven in the middle of a city, the entrance on a side street so discreet that it seemed these lovely gardens were not on the tourist trail. The layout was classic Japanese: pond, bridges, stone lanterns, pavilions, teahouses, cherry and plum trees. Some bossy signs told us which way to go, or not to tread on the moss, or rather more oddly: 'Don't Stay Here', and 'Be careful of the bee'.

We'd read about Kyoto's most famous Buddhist temple, Kiyomizu-dera, a magnificent structure on top of a hill overlooking the city, and about the ancient, winding lanes leading up to it. Don't always believe the guidebooks. The reality was a long, steep street of tourist tat and thousands of people. It seemed that nothing much had changed since celebrated master of haiku Matsuo Basho penned this in 1666:

from Kyoto's many houses
a crowd of ninety-nine thousand
blossom viewing

On our slow, hot ascent we paused for breath at a rather photogenic shrine (but at that time of year, no cherry blossom). We'd been getting sweaty and irritated as we climbed, but a sign at the shrine translated as 'Anger is strictly prohibited,' so we had to calm down. The Kiyomizu-dera temple and its hilltop setting were glorious, and the throng of Japanese visitors suggested there might have been a festival going on.

The view from the hill was less glorious. In recent decades developers have succeeded in defacing the old city skyline with ugly modern constructions. The train station, all steel and glass and very impressive from the inside, has been likened to a battleship, while the 1960s-era Kyoto Tower is a 'pinnacle of bad taste'. Although around two thousand temples and shrines still survive, many smaller wooden buildings have been demolished and replaced by apartment blocks. Spare a thought, then, for the Buddhist monks in that temple on the hill: they have always prayed outside every morning at dawn, looking down on the city in quiet contemplation, but nowadays it must be difficult for them to be Zen-like when faced with a battleship, a sea of concrete and a tacky 400-foot observation tower. Writer Jan Morris described Kyoto's many temples and shrines as 'scattered across the city like gems in mud', decrying the harsh juxtaposition of new and old as 'like a juke box in an abbey'. On the other hand, American author and Kyoto resident Alex Kerr had almost given up hope on his adopted city as a 'chaotic and trashy modern cityscape', but recently became more hopeful about preserving what is left, and the reason is tourism: 'Tourism has swept all before it...In fact, now it is the engine of whatever will be saved. Now the national imperative is tourism – from the prime minister down to the tiniest little village. It's the magic word, and that's good.'

As proof of this optimism, *Travel and Leisure* magazine has twice voted Kyoto the best city in the world to visit. Indeed, despite the modernisation you could easily spend a week there and get a real feel for traditional Japan – stay at an inn, bathe in hot springs, shop, tour the sights at a more leisurely pace and, importantly, hire a local guide to bridge the cultural gap. Unfortunately, being on a cruise ship made that impossible for us.

Back down the hill, we noticed a studio advertising a kind of be-a-geisha-for-the-day service. In the West, wear a kimono to a party and you may get accused of cultural appropriation, but here in Japan, for a fee, local businesses are happy to paint your face white and dress you up in their national costume for a photoshoot. Mrs V was not tempted.

The send-off from Kobe upped the ante somewhat, making Hakodate's ceremony look like a bunch of kindergartners. Cute kids doing a squid dance was not Kobe's style – here we had about thirty teenage girls lined up on the terminal balcony as though in a Rio carnival, smiling and waving to us, a riot of colour in their feather headdresses, bikini tops and frilly skirts, lacy gloves and a surprising amount of bare skin.

They were attracting a lot of attention from a dense group of mostly men on the balcony adjoining ours who started taking photographs, oblivious to us standing two feet away. To the right of the girls, inconspicuous in plain brown costumes but very audible, a *taiko* (Japanese drum) group was giving an outstanding display of synchronised drumming at high volume.

It's ironic that home-grown modernisation has destroyed parts of old Kyoto. In August 1945 the Americans' plan had been to drop the second atomic bomb on Kyoto but the city was spared when the Secretary of War, understanding its cultural importance, removed it from the target list. An alternative choice – Kokura – also escaped destruction, because on the day of the mission the town was obscured by smoke and the aircraft crew had orders only to release the bomb if their target was visible.

And so the pilot changed course for his alternative target.

Nagasaki

At 11:02 am on 9th August 1945 a B29 bomber from a US base in the Pacific dropped an atomic bomb on Nagasaki from an altitude of 30,000 feet. The bomb exploded above the city, causing about 74,000 deaths and a similar number injured, totalling two thirds of the population.

Along with some American passengers we took a tram out to Nagasaki's Peace Park, which commemorates the atomic bombing. Entering the park via an escalator flanked by flowers, we paused at a fountain where water jets were forming the shape of a dove's wings, and passed along an avenue of sculptures donated by various countries, each with a message of peace. We came to an elegant metal tower supporting a single bell, where people seemed to be lining up alongside a very long bell rope.

> • **Mrs Verne**: We left the ship a little later than intended but for that reason were lucky enough to arrive at the Peace Park just in time for a ceremony which takes place only on the 9th of each month at exactly 11:02. A bell is rung that has a rope long enough for a number of people to pull on together. Several very elderly Japanese men and women – clearly old enough to have experienced the bomb – motioned to us and our accompanying American friends to pull along with them to sound the bell. We were moved to tears.

At a nearby table, beneath a banner reading 'For Swift Abolition of Nuclear Weapons', a man handed out leaflets and asked people to sign a petition. Further into the Peace Park, a large paved square was dominated at the far end by a massive bronze sculpture of a man seated on a rock, right arm pointing to the sky, left arm held horizontally. 'The right hand points to the atomic bomb, the left hand points to peace, and the face prays deeply for the victims of war,' the sculptor had written below.

On either side of the statue were stone shrines housing strings and strings of tiny rainbow-coloured paper cranes, a reminder of the sad story of a two-year-old girl who survived Hiroshima but ten years later succumbed to leukaemia as a result of her exposure to radiation. After her diagnosis she remembered the ancient Japanese belief that anyone who folds a thousand origami cranes will see their wish come true, and set about the task in the hope of getting better. She died before reaching the thousand. Every year the peace memorials in Hiroshima and Nagasaki receive millions of origami cranes, from children inspired by her story.

While we were in the square several large groups of high-school-age children arrived, lined up neatly, listened to a guide or teacher and then had class photos taken. Smaller groups of elderly Japanese were also visiting and having their photos taken. It seemed a respectful rather than solemn occasion: the children were well behaved, the older men and women relaxed and smiling, as if meeting for a regular reunion – perhaps after being in the city together as young children in August 1945.

The Atomic Bomb Museum across the way was, as you would expect, graphic and harrowing. Alongside the photos, videos and exhibits, captions in English helped bring home the horror of what had happened. A darkened room contained items from that day, some dramatic, others poignant – a water tower on a twisted steel frame, blackened masonry and statues, melted bottles, broken clocks, a schoolgirl's charred lunch box, and the bones of a human hand fused with melted glass. It was a surprise to learn that eight thousand of the dead had belonged to Japan's oldest and largest Catholic community, which had grown out of centuries-old contact with missionaries and traders. But there was a bitter irony for Japanese Christians: both the pilot and the chaplain who had blessed the bombing raid were Catholic.

A short distance from the museum was the Hypocentre, a simple black plinth marking the point on the ground above which the bomb exploded.

After such a sombre morning, we spent a couple of hours enjoying the peaceful surroundings of Glover Garden, a 19th century merchant's residence on a hillside overlooking Nagasaki harbour. Thomas Glover, a Scot, played a key role in the industrialisation of Japan, including the establishment of what later turned into the Mitsubishi Corporation. His European colonial-style house and its location bring to mind the traditional type of setting for Puccini's *Madame Butterfly*, which takes place in Nagasaki. Although it did not directly inspire Puccini's opera, Glover Garden has made the most of the very tenuous connection by erecting a statue of the composer and a sculpture of a Japanese diva famed for playing the role, while the gift shop sells a range of Madame Butterfly perfumes and creams. In the opera, Butterfly is overjoyed when she spies the arrival of an American ship carrying her husband, Lieutenant Pinkerton, who has been away for three years. Now, from the very same hill (or not, but let's pretend), we too were pretty pleased to see an American-flagged ship at anchor in the harbour, as it meant that the *Amsterdam* had not left without us. We made our way down to rejoin our ship and say goodbye to Japan.

A youth orchestra on the quayside played as we sailed away. According to Murray's Handbook, girls of that age in 1907 would not be serenading ships in the harbour but hauling sacks of coals for them. It stated admiringly that

...a notable feature of the harbour is the coaling of steamers by gangs of young girls, who pass small baskets from hand to hand with amazing rapidity. One of the Empress steamers has had 1,210 tons of coal put on board in this way in 3 1/4 hours!

PART II: South Korea to Indonesia

SOUTH KOREA: Jeju City, Jeju Island

And yet the sea is a terrible place, stupefying to the mind and poisonous to the temper, the sea, the motion, the lack of space, the cruel publicity, the villainous tinned foods, the sailors, the captain, the passengers – but you are amply repaid when you sight an island, and drop anchor in a new world.

(Robert Louis Stevenson, letter from Tahiti)

Jeju Island lies fifty miles off the tip of South Korea, between Japan and China. Cruise line websites paint an idyllic picture: 'Blessed with tangerine groves, swaying palm trees, white sand beaches, and a verdant landscape, Korea's southernmost volcanic island has long been a favored holiday and honeymoon retreat.' HAL was offering a few excursions for our brief visit, including a 'folk village', a temple, a museum, or some volcanic rocks. For many ports HAL advertises the option of a private minivan for a full day. For Jeju City, a large minivan was a reasonable $US 85 per person, a smaller vehicle less so ($200 pp). There was a private car option too, at $400 pp. (Incredibly, a private car tour in Nagasaki would have been $900 pp.) No meals or entrance fees were included for any of these private tours. The large minivan may be the cheapest but spare a thought for the passenger organising it, who has to find a dozen other occupants, collect payments, reach a consensus on the itinerary and then try to keep order during the day as half the group start changing their minds about where to go and the other half argue about when to stop for lunch.

As so often, we chose not to fork out on a ship's excursion or private tour but to wander at will and soak up some local colour. The city was fairly uninspiring at first but we soon found a lively market, its entrance flanked by two stone 'grandfathers', eight-foot-high figures carved from basalt and symbols of protection and fertility. The market had immaculate displays of red and yellow citrus fruits, sacks of spices and neat rows of fresh seafood, while the live fish in tanks and pigs' heads on tables were a novelty to us, accustomed as we are to seeing our food packaged with barely a hint of the animal it came from.

Not far from the market were some reconstructions of ancient government buildings, which sounds dull but the beauty of the ornately carved and colourfully decorated wooden structures was a revelation. We had never seen municipal buildings quite like these before. Originally built in 1435, they were completely destroyed by the Japanese during their 'Colonial Occupation' of

Korea from 1910 to 1945, and not reconstructed until the early 2000s.

The occupiers had used the population as slave labour, suppressed their culture and introduced compulsory military service ('to do justice to the patriotic spirit of the Koreans', as the Japanese government put it). As we wandered and read about the history of the buildings, it was obvious from several pointed references that the Japanese occupation had not been forgotten.

An inscription on the monument to a popular 19th-century governor hinted at a more lyrical side to the Korean language than we had seen so far on the rather dry, factual signs around the site:

He governed Jeju Island as perfect as cooking a fish.

We are pleased as a duck with his glory.

There is said to be a poetry to the island and its people, an other-worldliness not apparent to the casual honeymooner or cruise passenger. French/Mauritian writer JMG Le Clézio, a longtime admirer and now honorary citizen of Jeju, has written eloquently about it: traces of ghosts and spirits are everywhere, he says – by the roadside, on rocks, in fields. The sea is populated with mermaids who are ruled by the dragon king, and the rivers are home to fairies 'who can sometimes be spotted early in the morning in their foggy capes'. But of Jeju's many mythological figures the stone grandfathers are the most visible, standing ready to repel all invaders (if apparently powerless against the hordes of tourists).

We wandered around looking for a place to have lunch, but the smaller cafés had Korean-only menus and seating was on the floor. The harbour was lined with more restaurants, each boasting an array of fish tanks out front, and although one or two had menus in English we could not pluck up the courage to enter. 'Boiled down rainbowfish', 'shredded coral fish ice soup' and 'raw filefish' just weren't enough to entice us in. Somewhat disconsolately, we arrived back at the modern hotel where the ship's shuttle bus had dropped us earlier and were relieved to see that they had their own restaurant, with regular tables and chairs, and a menu in English that did not involve the shredding of exotic fish from the nearby coral reef. We had delicious yet spicy kimchi followed by a very welcome juicy tangerine, an island speciality. For some reason, the restaurant was completely empty – the locals might not come here, but where were the tourists? We suspected that many from the *Amsterdam,* if not on a tour, had taken the easy option and returned to the ship for a free lunch of familiar dull food. We may have failed to go to an authentic eatery, but at least we were trying the cuisine and contributing something to the island's economy.

> • **Mrs Verne again:** Judging from our red faces and streaming eyes, the hotel's kimchi casserole with black pork and Chinese cabbage was very authentic indeed.

Back at the quayside, a lady from the tourist board asked us some questions – where had we gone, did we like Jeju, had we bought any souvenirs? I say with some satisfaction, given the usual eye-rolling from my spouse on this subject, that the lady was pretty impressed when I showed her the bookmark I had bought printed with the Korean alphabet. As a reward, she gave me two miniature plastic grandfathers.

Between most ports of call there was a day or two at sea. We started to watch the interviews that the cruise director did with a new guest every morning on TV, usually an entertainer, lecturer, officer, or other crew member. The light-hearted chat would cover their career and background, or give an insight into life behind the scenes on a cruise ship, and occasionally this prompted us to go to a show or lecture we hadn't thought of attending. Even if not, it was often an interesting half hour. One officer described the steps that HAL and other cruise lines were taking to go green: plugging into a port's local power rather than spewing diesel fumes, recycling plastic and glass, converting salt water to drinking water, developing biofuels from plant and fish waste, and so on. We were sceptical, cruise ships being notorious polluters, but maybe the combination of new technologies and tougher laws is nudging the industry slowly in the right direction. There were paper straws instead of plastic on our cruise, so that's a start.

We did try a couple of what were billed as free consultations. With the daily programme cajoling us to 'come along this morning for a free footprint and posture analysis!' we were persuaded to visit the very alien world of the gym, where an enthusiastic young staff member got us to stand in bare feet on an inked pad and then explained that we would need special shoe inserts to correct an imbalance, which, strangely, we both seemed to have. Luckily, he said, they had some in stock. Reasoning that a lack of balance is to be expected on a ship at sea, we declined. (According to one online comment, the only thing they're analysing is 'whether you are gullible enough to buy $US 300 orthotic inserts from a cruise ship spa'.)

Then there were the tanzanite seminars. Basically sales pitches with free bubbly, they are a feature of every cruise we've ever been on, which is odd for an allegedly rare gemstone mined solely from one area of Mount Kilimanjaro. What did we learn? Well, though beautiful, tanzanite is a poor choice for rings or bracelets as it can easily chip and even crack; vinegar or lemon juice may cause irreparable damage; and to achieve that lovely rich blue colour, the stones – brownish in their natural state – have to be heat treated, which is not fraudulent but does lower their value. No, *of course* they don't say any of this in the seminars: I got it from reading an insurance underwriter's sober advice to agents in the industry, which concluded that 'any jewelry marketed to tourists may be overpriced or misrepresented, so the insurer should be wary of insuring such purchases'. So think carefully before impulse buying.

Sea days are also a chance to meet new people over lunch. Some you might be on a wavelength with, others less so. On this leg of the cruise we once shared a table with a couple who were good company – intelligent and engaging, just like us. The woman, who was black, said that someone had recently refused to sit next to her in the dining room, though this was an isolated incident.

On another day, a man revealed he was single and travelling alone, at which one of the ladies around the table perked up and commented that he'd be looking for a girlfriend then. 'That's making a big assumption,' Mrs V muttered to him, and he nodded in agreement. Then there was the poor guy with dementia who repeated the same thing several times, but as it was so clearly a relief for his wife to share the burden we were happy to chat with him. Another man told us he had served on P&O liners in the 1950s and was happy to be the one sitting down.

A more lively social event on some cruises is the 'cabin crawl', which is a good way to make new friends but also to have a nose round other people's staterooms while imbibing their alcohol. A crawl is normally arranged by a Cruise Critic roll call member, who maps out the route and aims for everyone to end up in one of the larger suites (preferably with butler service). Each host provides the drinks and snacks, and decorates the cabin – it's like going to six parties in one evening. Those who stay the course then tend to stagger along to the casino for a 'slot pull', taking it in turns to pull the handle of a one-armed bandit in the hopes of a payout. I have to say that though we went for drinks or a meal with other couples more than a few times, we never did a cabin crawl, which personally I feel very aggrieved about.

- **Mrs Verne**: He wasn't allowed. Might get out of hand.

CHINA: Beijing

But that's the glory of foreign travel, as far as I am concerned. I don't want to know what people are talking about. I can't think of anything that excites a greater sense of childlike wonder than to be in a country where you are ignorant of almost everything... Your whole existence becomes a series of interesting guesses.

(Bill Bryson, *Neither Here Nor There*)

On the long drive back to port at the end of our two-day stop in Beijing, our taxi driver spoke no English and we had no idea where we were as we passed endless rows of identical apartment blocks in featureless suburbs. We hadn't been at all sure he understood where we wanted to go. Anxiously checking my watch, I realised that by this time the ship would already have sailed without us. This was no 'interesting guess'. This was stomach-churning, heart-sinking, catastrophic reality.

Of that, more later. But first, how we fared in Beijing.

After South Korea, the *Amsterdam* was due to dock for two days in the port of Tianjin, 110 miles from Beijing, so to make the most of our time in the capital and avoid time-wasting back-and-forth journeys we had booked a hotel in Beijing for an overnight stay. Brave Mrs V was suffering from a heavy cold and a mouth ulcer but was determined to miss nothing. Getting there under our own steam proved to be our biggest challenge yet, however. Once in port we set out, armed with little more than a card issued by the ship listing a few places of interest in Chinese and some currency conversions. Banding together with two or three other intrepid passengers, we soon discovered that everything our onboard travel expert had told us was wrong, and there was much confusion at the little local railway station as all signs were in Chinese only and the staff did not speak English. We somehow managed to pay for tickets and find the right train to the far larger Tianjin city railway station, then boarded the express to Beijing. From the train we peered through smog at a relentless procession of tall apartment blocks, many of them still under construction.

Finally, after another taxi ride, we arrived at our Beijing hotel around 1pm, a modern building near the Forbidden City on a quiet, tree-lined street filled with birdsong, though the birds were in fact for sale in cages across the road. Our en suite bathroom had glass walls and no door (it was a 'boutique' hotel – what else did we expect?). At least there were curtains you could pull. But we had no time to lose, and managed to arrange at very short notice a trip to the Great Wall, hiring a driver via the hotel reception for about $US 130 / £95. He didn't speak any English, but most importantly he got us to the wall after only an hour or so by driving fast and dangerously, weaving between the many large, slow-moving trucks that belched noxious fumes into the open windows of our non-air-conditioned car. As PJ O'Rourke joked: 'The English drive on the left. The Americans drive on the right. The Chinese respect both customs.'

We were visiting the part of the wall nearest to Beijing – Badaling, a fully restored section known for being very crowded, but we had no choice as our time was so limited. Here's American columnist Tom Scocca's description of Badaling:

At last, past yet more poncho vendors, we reached it: the parking lot. Oh, and behind it, up the rise, there was the Great Wall, too. But first there were the buses, and the people getting off the buses, and then rows of stalls full of Great Wall knickknacks and Great Wall books and Great Wall T-shirts, with customers swarming the doorways. The people streamed up into the visitors' center, where they filled a round theater to watch a 360-degree panoramic movie of the Great Wall.

(Tom Scocca, *Beijing Welcomes You*)

And yet, possibly because it was mid October, Badaling was not at all crowded that day and there was no sign of the aggressive peddlers of tourist tat we'd been led to expect. The few visitors there seemed Chinese, as Scocca had also noted ('Chinese vendors selling Chinese-made kitsch to Chinese sightseers').

When Richard Nixon came here in 1972 he declared it 'a great wall' – a much-mocked soundbite, though to be fair he did add 'and it had to be built by a great people'. 'Built by a great number of slave labourers' would have been more accurate, but less diplomatic. (In fact, the Great Wall consists of several walls constructed over many centuries, and has never been a continuous structure. It didn't take much tactical genius for Genghis Khan to lead his hordes through a wide gap and capture Beijing in 1215.)

Chairman Mao famously decreed that climbing the Wall would make you a hero, but we opted instead for the rickety cable car up to the top, and spent the next hour or so walking along its battlements and enjoying wonderful views. The massive wall with its regularly spaced watchtowers snaked up and down for many miles, glowing in the afternoon sun, while away to the west mountain ridges lined the horizon in hazy silhouette (air pollution again, no doubt). Hidden speakers in the trees below blared out a constant commentary in Chinese, and songs that might have inspired us to march more determinedly up the steeper parts of the wall if only we had understood the lyrics.

Back in Beijing that evening we experienced the best and worst of Chinese cuisine. On the recommendation of the hotel's concierge, we went to a restaurant specialising in Peking Duck. Very obviously aimed at tourists, they put on quite a show with the chef at a table out front carving up whole ducks.

- **Mrs Verne again:** There was a little incident at the restaurant that Mr Verne would like me to draw a veil over but I'm not going to. While we were waiting for our order I suddenly felt very faint in the heat and went out into the hall to get some air. Sitting there in a chair – gaped at by strangers – I think I blacked out for a second but luckily came to very quickly. 'It's OK, I just came over a little faint but I'm better now,' I reassured Mr Verne when I went back in. 'Oh, did you go somewhere?' he asked through a mouthful of duck. Reader, while I lay unconscious and perhaps only minutes away from an uncertain fate, he didn't even notice I was missing.

I would like to point out, in mitigation, that an assistant chef had been demonstrating something very important: how to combine the various items on our plate before eating. Lay out the pancake, dip two or three pieces of duck into the sauce, place on pancake, add onion and cucumber, and wrap neatly into a parcel. You had to concentrate, or get it in the wrong order. 'Neatly' we did not manage, but it was still delicious.

 Anyway, on the way back to the hotel (in a frosty silence) we passed through the celebrated Wangfujing Market where a long line of stalls sold a nightmarish array of supposedly edible creepy-crawlies on sticks: birds, spiders, grasshoppers, scorpions, silk-worms, snakes and giant centipedes were all carefully skewered and laid out for late-night snacking. We were not tempted, and neither were any of the other strolling tourists as far as we could see.

The day may be approaching when insects will be bred globally for cheap, protein-rich food, but Western palates will surely only find insects acceptable if they are pulverised into oblivion and then mixed in with other foodstuffs – out of mind unless you look more closely at the list of ingredients and spot the centipede extract. Depending how hungry we all get, of course. Then we'll eat anything.

Beijing had undergone a remarkable transformation in recent decades. Hosting the Olympic Games in 2008 had been a chance for the country to prove to the world that its capital was a modern, forward-looking metropolis. Many of the old neighbourhoods were bulldozed to make way for brutal new buildings, wider roads, an airport terminal, and that express train between Beijing and Tianjin. In the build-up to the Games and its expected flood of foreign visitors, the authorities had aspired to teach a third of residents to speak some English. They also tried to get everyone to stop spitting in public and learn how to queue nicely at bus stops and ticket windows, rather than the usual free-for-all (special 'line-up days' were mandated for the locals to practise queuing). Now, years later, it seemed to us that traditional Chinese culture was still wonderfully untainted by such alien Western habits.

But we were here to see what was left of the old China, and especially the Forbidden City. As a symbol of the imperial past, the 600-year-old emperor's palace narrowly escaped demolition by the communists in the 1950s, but nowadays its preservation is assured as a must-see tourist attraction. Next morning we set out early – well, nine o'clockish, and only after coffee at the hotel, obviously – for an eagerly anticipated visit.

Once inside, we slowly made our way up through the vast centre of the City, comprising a series of large wooden halls on raised white marble platforms, each one separated by a plaza of parade ground proportions.

It was easy to avoid the crowds when crossing these acres of stone plaza, but the halls created bottlenecks where a dense crush of people would funnel up the steps and jostle to get a look in, then go down the other side to look for fellow tour group members in baseball caps the same colour as their own.

The biggest and most important pavilion, the Hall of Supreme Harmony, traditionally used for imperial enthronement and wedding ceremonies, was restored in 2008. The exterior paintwork was magnificent. We had been impressed by the beautifully decorated government buildings on South Korea's Jeju Island, but this Ming bling was positively dazzling: saffron-yellow roof tiles, walls of vermilion red, countless painted dragons, and intricate geometrical patterns all glistening in the sunshine. However, entry into the Hall was not allowed and we could barely see anything in the gloomy interior (and presumably neither could the more pushy tour group members who fought their way to the front).

Bernardo Bertolucci's movie *The Last Emperor* (1987) was the first Western film authorised to be shot inside the Forbidden City. External scenes were done in the vast squares, complete with 19,000 extras, but only one internal scene was permitted – that of the infant Puyi being crowned as the new emperor in the Hall of Supreme Harmony, filmed by just one cameraman and no lighting equipment because the Chinese authorities were so afraid of fire risk. All other internal scenes were shot on specially constructed sound stages. The little boy playing the emperor-to-be – a native Californian, incidentally – had to be coaxed with the promise of rewards. Director Bertolucci explained:

He hears the sound of a cricket in the courtyard among the courtesans and he goes around looking for it. We challenged him to look for this cricket like it was a game and he would get a reward for finding it. We had to keep giving the boy rewards. I said I'd take him up on the crane and after that he did everything. He liked to look through the viewfinder and ride in the crane. So we let him do whatever he wanted.

On either side of the immense halls and squares we found some relief from the crowds in a confusing maze of alleys, courtyards and smaller structures, which included the private quarters of the emperor and his entourage, 'rooms haunted by the shuffle and gossip of seventy thousand eunuchs and the yawns of concubines', in the words of travel writer Colin Thubron. We learned that desperately poor farmers in the provinces would castrate their sons and send them to the capital in the hope they would be taken on as eunuch guards or servants and earn money to support their family. Another story concerned the emperor's belief that the best way for him to build up enough potency to father an heir was to have lots of sex with his concubines – but without consummating the act. He could then absorb plenty of female life force while also storing up his own 'energy' in preparation for his monthly tryst with the empress. That was the theory. Unsurprisingly, emperors did not always restrain themselves and male heirs were sometimes born to a favoured concubine.

We ambled around these more intimate parts of the City, from the Lodge of Spiritual Cultivation, past the Hall of Abstinence, glancing wistfully at the Palace of Benevolent Tranquillity – just the place for a nice sit down, we thought – and finally to the Palace of Eternal Longevity. As for the palaces of Tranquil Longevity and Joyful Longevity and the rest of the 800 or so buildings in the palace complex, enough was enough. Seriously flagging by this point, we gratefully followed signs to the Palace Museum Tea House and the Palace of Joyful Toilets. (I may have made up that last one.)

A branch of Starbucks opened in the Forbidden City in 2000, greeted by a public outcry at this perceived threat to Chinese culture, and a petition with half a million signatures later succeeded in getting the outlet removed. It may seem surprising that a Starbucks was ever allowed to open in such a showcase for the nation's heritage, but money was inevitably involved: rent from the shop funded some of the palace renovations. In any case, we enjoyed a refreshing all-Chinese cup of tea in the more culturally appropriate Tea House and moved on to the gift shop. In hindsight, this marked the point at which our day began to unravel, little frustrations leading to larger ones and stress levels rising until the awful dénouement several hours later.

At the gift shop, we settled on some inexpensive souvenirs: embroidered carp dancing in a circle, watercolours of lotus flowers, and – yes – a bookmark. A haggling technique recommended to us for China had been to offer 30% of the asking price and work up from there, but being British I timidly offered 80% straight away. I got nowhere and ended up paying full price.

A journey is like marriage. The certain way to be wrong is to think you control it.

(John Steinbeck, *Travels with Charley*)

We wanted to go to Tiananmen Square next, but as this was back where we had started hours ago on the far side of the Forbidden City, we left by the northern gate and engaged a cycle rickshaw rather than a boring old taxi. The rickshaw being a single-seater, or at least not wide enough for two Westerners, we had to hire his friend's rickshaw too. Off we went through a bewildering labyrinth of little alleys, and although we were having fun I was slightly nervous that we were intermittently out of sight of each other. Our cyclists were small but pretty fit and pedalled hard, but then suddenly they halted we knew not where, gestured that Tiananmen Square was nearby, and demanded an extortionate amount of money. I protested, then tried to bargain, but of course to no avail. Walking away from these surly toughs was probably not a sensible option, and no police were around, so I coughed up. The penny finally dropped: we had been shanghaied in Beijing.

Now on foot and (possibly) heading for Tiananmen we stopped at a shop to buy a T-shirt for our son. The price was 80 yuan, I offered 50, and the female shop assistant laughed at me. By now pretty fed up, I turned and stomped off down the street. Mrs V and the vendor eventually emerged and beckoned, but I stood my ground so that they had to come to me. Now *both* of them seemed to find my behaviour amusing, but at least the girl did agree to 50 yuan. If that's haggling, forget it.

In Tiananmen Square, under the watchful eye of blank-faced guards, we paid our respects to the huge portrait of the Great Helmsman Chairman Mao, founding father of modern China who died in 1976. His face also appears on banknotes, and souvenir shops do a good trade in Mao statues, posters and mugs. In the middle of the square was Mao's mausoleum, where thousands usually queue to file past his embalmed body (or perhaps a wax replica), his role in the death of millions officially erased from the national memory. We did not line up: we had a ship to catch. With only a little time to spare for a quick lunch, we stopped at a restaurant full of local diners. Not tempted by their 'delicious chicken saliva' special, we ordered a vegetarian dish and some drinking water from a waitress who spoke no English. She brought a jug of *hot* water and disappeared for twenty minutes, so we gave up and left, hungry.

Things were going downhill fast. Ripped off by undersized cyclists, laughed at by a girl, and now ignored in a restaurant – could my fragile male ego stand much more of this? At the hotel we took a taxi and then the express train back to Tianjin. So far, so good – just another 35 miles to the port. But then came a really serious problem: there were no onward trains until 17:30, the very time we had to be back at the ship, or else. Now what? The bus station was just across the way, but proved to have no information in English. Another taxi was our only hope.

A young woman approached and asked in halting English if we needed help, and of course we were desperately grateful, having learnt in the last twenty-four hours that a knowledge of English seemed pretty rare in this part of China. After speaking to a couple of taxi drivers nearby, she concluded alarmingly that it was too dangerous to go with either one, and led us down a ramp into the bowels of the train station where the official taxi rank was. Despite this apparently obvious solution to our problem, it still took several minutes of half-understood back and forth between the woman, the taxi dispatcher and ourselves to agree destination and price. We were relying solely on our little card in Chinese to convey the location of the ship, and were by no means certain the driver understood either that or the urgency required. With no other choice, we set off and for the next hour or so passed through those endless, identical-looking high-rise suburbs, unable to read any road signs or talk to the driver and getting more and more tense at every red traffic light.

Finally, after a wrong turn into a yard full of shipping containers, we came upon a more likely dock entrance, rounded a corner and there was the wonderful, wonderful *Amsterdam*. The driver sped across the concrete expanse, spurred on by our excitement, and we started to relax as we saw a bus disgorging passengers at the quayside. Although clearly past the 'all aboard' deadline the ship had not sailed, apparently because an official excursion had also been late back – the only instance when they will wait. This lucky coincidence had saved us from disaster. A few ironic cheers wafted down from an upper deck as we made our way up the gangway. We flopped onto our bunks in the utmost relief and listened to passenger names being paged over the tannoy, a sure sign that some had still not returned (and, it was rumoured later, three couples had indeed been stranded ashore). Our fellow diners greeted us that evening with raucous applause as we entered. Aussie friends Paul and Karen said they had gone up to the top deck, cocktails in hand, to look out for our return (or not).

> • **Mrs Verne here:** I thought that sounded suspiciously like they might have been celebrating the chance never to see us again.

If only we had heeded the chinahighlights.com website, which advises on the pros and cons of travelling between Tianjin and Beijing. The do-it-yourself method can be expensive, navigation is difficult and you should bargain in Mandarin, they say, and is therefore not recommended, whereas pre-booked private transfers have the advantages of an English-speaking guide, no hassles and the peace of mind from returning five hours before your cruise departs.

But where's the fun in that?

While aboard the *Amsterdam* we learned that its 'godmother' (the person who christened the ship) was Janet Lanterman, wife of the then CEO of Holland America. A name familiar enough in HAL circles, and no doubt a very nice lady, but perhaps lacking the cachet of some more famous godmothers over the years. Many HAL ships have been christened by members of the Dutch royal family, but not the *Amsterdam*, while our very own Queen Elizabeth christened three of Cunard's ships. And if you couldn't get the Queen, the next best was actress Helen Mirren, who played the title role in the movie *The Queen*: Helen christened P&O's *Ventura* in 2008, aided by two Royal Marine commandos who abseiled down and smashed champagne bottles against the hull. Judi Dench – more British acting royalty – was godmother to *Carnival Legend*, but only managed to break the bottle at her third attempt, completely soaking herself in the process and earning the entirely predictable tabloid headline 'Now It's Dame Judi Drench!'. The choice for *Disney Wonder* was the fairy Tinker Bell, who fluttered along the side of the ship with the aid of laser projection, her speech translated by Mickey Mouse. But the prize for glamour and brand loyalty goes to Italian film icon Sophia Loren, who is godmother to an entire fleet – at least seventeen MSC ships. No messy bottle smashing for Ms Loren, though: at her ceremonies she just flashes her dazzling smile and cuts a ribbon.

Cruise companies chase movie stars for their glamour, but it also works in reverse, as the movies have regularly featured cruise ships and luxury liners. But you could count on one hand those that used actual ships, as opposed to only studio sets or models. *Out to Sea* (1997), shot on HAL's *Westerdam,* was a comedy starring Jack Lemmon and Walter Matthau as dance hosts on a cruise ship ('it's our job to flirt with all the classy broads', explains Matthau's character). Some of the passengers who volunteered as extras became bored with rehearsals and endless takes, often sneaking off so as not to miss bingo or happy hour, and so professional actors had to be brought in from Los Angeles to solve the problem.

By contrast, when during a *QM2* transatlantic crossing in 2019 a call went out for any budding actors to appear as extras in the filming of *Let Them All Talk,* hundreds of volunteers (attention seekers) came forward, eager to share the stage with its star, Meryl Streep. After the film was released old Cunard hands enjoyed spotting areas of the ship so familiar to them, but they were also quick to point out a 'major blooper' – Streep's friend (played by Candice Bergen) dines in the exclusive Queens Grill despite not occupying a suite, which of course is a shocking infringement of the Cunard class system. The film itself was deemed 'too talky'.

James Cameron's 1997 *Titanic* did feature the original ship, albeit briefly. At the start of the movie we see footage of the wreck, taken when Cameron – himself a keen diver – led a 1995 expedition to explore the remains using two Russian deep-sea submersibles, though even here some of the shots feature a scale model of a section of rusting hull. The big-budget 1980 movie *Raise The Titanic* had to use a model because the wreck's position was still unknown then; it bombed at the box office, causing producer Lew Grade to comment that it would have been cheaper to lower the Atlantic.

Of the dozen or so movies about the *Titanic* up to the present day, only one other could claim a real-life connection to the disaster: a ten-minute silent short, *Saved from the Titanic*, came out just a month after the 1912 disaster, starring Dorothy Gibson, a 22-year-old actress who actually survived the sinking. Dorothy's affecting performance, playing herself and wearing the same clothes as on the night the ship went down, was an instant hit, though the movie studio's rush to cash in was of questionable taste. No copies of *Saved from the Titanic* are known to have survived. But, just as the wreck of the *Titanic* was eventually found, so maybe a copy of the film will turn up one day and we will get to see the very first example of that enduring love affair between luxury liners and the silver screen.

Shanghai

After two days at sea the *Amsterdam* reached Shanghai in the early hours, and by the time we opened our curtains we could look down onto a little park where a few locals were already going through their daily tai chi ritual while others stopped to gaze up at the foreign object now blocking the view. We were berthed on the busy Huangpu River in the centre of the city, just a short walk from the Bund, a colonial-era waterfront promenade.

But before setting off to explore we had something more urgent to attend to. Before leaving the UK we had heeded writer Dervla Murphy's advice for older people about to travel:

One should avoid, for as long as possible, casual visits to the doctor. He/she is too likely to take blood samples, diagnose problems you haven't yet noticed, prescribe medicines that benefit only Big Pharma and advise you not to go where you want to go.

Once you hit the road, though, your continued health and wealth come down to plain luck and insurance policy small print. Mrs V now found herself in a dental agony impossible to ignore any longer, and the ship made an appointment for her at an international clinic in Shanghai and laid on a driver. Everything went smoothly, if expensively (but the insurance company later coughed up). The official driver to the dentist cost us $US 50 cash, whereas getting from the clinic to the city centre under our own steam, via taxi and metro train, totalled just $3.50.

> • **Mrs V:** I seem to make a habit of dental emergencies on cruise ships, even though I always get my teeth thoroughly overhauled beforehand. Nowadays, based on bitter experience, I come prepared with several courses of antibiotics and one of those little do-it-yourself dental first aid kits. If there was anything legal that would knock me out cold at the height of one of those agonizing tooth infections I'd be packing that too. There's no dentist on a cruise ship.

We were cruising the Nanjing Road shops by noon, but lunch was our priority and we rejected the upscale options in favour of a very basic eatery down a side street where no foreigners were to be seen. The large, laminated menu was in Chinese and a kind of English; faced with dishes such as 'The sun purifies big lake brake crab', 'Get rid of small lobster of head', and 'Duck blood cake', we opted for the more familiar Shanghai speciality: meat-filled dumplings and noodles. Only then did we go to survey the city's spectacular riverside setting. The Bund – a Hindi word for embankment – is a mile-long curve of waterfront lined with imposing neoclassical buildings, built in the 19th century when the British, French and Americans set up their banks and trading houses after the Chinese were 'persuaded' to allow foreign trade. One such bank is the magnificent Hong

Kong and Shanghai Banking Corporation (HSBC) Building, which is a major bank in the UK but with a poor reputation, having supported Beijing's draconian anti-protest law in Hong Kong and been fined for tax evasion and accepting cash from Mexican drug cartels. I have an account with them, just in case I need to launder some money some day, no questions asked.

From the Bund we watched a constant parade of buzzing little tour boats, container ships gliding up the river, and cruise ships docking nearby (or at least the smaller ones, as larger vessels have to tie up 15 miles away). Across the river is the ultra-modern Pudong financial district with its forest of gleaming skyscrapers. Both sides of the river and all the boats are lit up at night, and from the decks of the *Amsterdam* we had a perfect view.

Explorer Isabella Bird described Shanghai in 1897 as the 'London of the Pacific' for its commerce and gaiety, but by the 1930s the city had become so disreputable that it gained a new nickname – the 'Paris of the East'. There was no sign of vice in the old town behind the Bund as we continued our tour of world religions by visiting the City God Temple, which is Taoist. Like Shintoism in Japan, Taoism features a huge pantheon of gods, and indeed the walls of one room were lined with statues of scary deities in glass cabinets. A mother and her little boy knelt in prayer to an impressively red-faced, bushy-bearded City God, who it seems had been a mere mortal (a boring old civil servant like us) until posthumously anointed as a god.

The beautifully tended gardens at the Confucian Temple were an oasis of tranquillity, unlike the heaving mass of humanity at the similar, but far more popular, Yu Yuan Gardens. Not surprisingly, being cruisers with little time ashore (and, frankly, little in the way of spiritual depth) we gained no real insights into Buddhism, Shintoism, Taoism or Confucianism while touring the East. Nice gardens, though.

We split up on the second afternoon, me to explore with my camera, Mrs V to shop. No one took any notice of me as I wandered the narrow lanes, but on my way back along the Bund to the ship I was approached by three young women who asked me to take photos, then chatted about Shanghai and invited me to a 'cultural festival'. I smelled a rat from the start, of course – they were very charming, but I'm not that stupid – and declined. As I discovered later, the *Rough Guide to Shanghai* has this warning about scam artists:

Commonly, a sweet-looking young couple, a pair of girls, or perhaps a kindly old man, will ask to practise their English or offer to show you round. After befriending you – which may take hours – they will suggest some refreshment, and lead you to a teahouse. Following a traditional-looking tea ceremony you will be presented with a bill for thousands of yuan, your new 'friends' will disappear or pretend to be shocked, and some large gentlemen will appear.

I can't account for what happened to us the day before, though, in the same area of the city. As we strolled along we noticed a young man secretly taking a photo of his friend walking next to Mrs V, and then perhaps more bizarrely, a few minutes later a man in office clothes asked to have his photo taken with me. I cautiously agreed, keeping one hand on my wallet as I smiled for the camera. So, what was going on here: were we interesting foreigners, or ugly tall freaks to laugh about with their friends? Don't answer that.

Hong Kong

After Shanghai my back went very stiff (an old problem), which meant that if I sat anywhere for a while it was agony to haul myself up and start moving again. Embarrassingly, with dinners taking a couple of hours, I had to be manhandled out of my seat at the end of every evening by the waiter and our friend Paul, and only managed to straighten again once we reached our cabin, at which point I needed to lie down.

At Hong Kong the *Amsterdam* hove to and came alongside. Or perhaps it was the other way round. As in Shanghai, the cruise terminal was in a spectacular setting, and from the dockside in Kowloon we enjoyed wide-open views of busy Victoria Harbour and easy access to shops and ferry boats. Uncertain of what we could achieve here with a sudden mobility problem, we stepped ashore and made our way slowly through the terminal and adjoining mall. Breaking free from vendors offering fake Rolexes and Gucci handbags, we then found ourselves in the concrete jungle of Canton Road, where designer stores sold the real thing at outrageous prices. The stiffness in my back easing as I walked, we soon retreated from the crowds and noise to Kowloon Park, a walled, shaded sanctuary of winding paths, a lake with carp and turtles, a pagoda, and Kung Fu Corner (all quiet that day, unfortunately). Locals sweated up a steep 'fitness path' as we strolled down it. I checked out a viewpoint on a hill, which was less interesting for its hazy vista of skyscrapers than for the man silently going through his tai chi routine close by. As I dutifully took photos of the skyscrapers he just as silently appeared right at my elbow and gestured towards the haze. 'Pollution from the north,' he commented, obviously alluding discreetly to Beijing's increasing interference in Hong Kong's internal affairs, and hinting that things had been better under the British. At least I'm sure that's what he meant to convey.

A few remnants of British colonial presence lingered on: Kowloon Park was built on the site of an army barracks, a couple of its blocks now museums and its gun batteries converted into a children's playground.

Two antique cannon still remained on a hill, aimed threateningly at the entrance to Victoria Harbour in the direction of the *Amsterdam* lying innocently at anchor.

Hong Kong, at the tip of the Chinese mainland, has three main districts – New Territories to the north, Kowloon in the middle, then Hong Kong Island, the historic centre of the old British colony. Conveniently, the Star Ferry Pier was a short walk away from the ship, tickets to Hong Kong Island just $US 2 each. We set off across the harbour on the *Twinkling Star*, an iconic 1950s-era ferry boat with a green-and-cream trim, upper and lower wooden-planked decks and gently curved profile – the kind of little boat you loved to play with at bathtime (and maybe still do). Apart from stunning views of skyscraper-lined Victoria Harbour, there was plenty of activity on the water, though the only traditional wooden boat we could see was a large junk running a busy schedule of harbour cruises for tourists. Once ashore on Hong Kong Island, we took a taxi up to The Peak, savoured the incredible view back towards Kowloon and strolled along the quiet roads way above the bustle at sea level. We descended on the Peak Tram, an extremely steep funicular railway and an unforgettable experience, unless of course you keep your eyes closed throughout like Mrs V.

Back on the *Amsterdam*, once I'd been winched painfully out of my seat after dinner, we uncharacteristically graced the evening show with our presence. We were tempted out of our cabin by the news that a local troupe was coming on board to present a Cultural Arts Show. The performance was everything you would expect – traditional Chinese music, ribbon dancing, a lively dragon – but there was only one star of the show for me, a master of an art that I did not even know existed: face-changing. Masked, dressed in a voluminous cloak and sporting two huge insect antennae, the Master strode about the stage and time after time, with a wave of his cloak or a shake of the head, he would suddenly be wearing a completely new mask. However he made the switches, they were faster than the eye could see and always drew gasps and applause. The image of a cloaked, face-changing insect man is now forever lodged in my brain.

We returned to Hong Kong Island next day and took a bus over to the town of Stanley, passing pretty coastal scenery and well-to-do residential areas. The only poor housing we saw were some shacks which, we were told, had protected status as the last remnants of the old Hong Kong. Stanley itself turned out to be a tourist hotspot, teeming with tourists like us. The town had a couple of nice sandy beaches, a pleasant promenade, some bars, and a market selling the obligatory chopsticks, mahjong sets and lanterns. Restaurants varied – you could have fish and chips and a pint of Heineken at, say, The Smugglers Inn, but native dishes were also available elsewhere for the more adventurous, of whom there seemed few. For the truly unimaginative, there was of course a McDonald's, right next to Starbucks.

Local colour could be found a short way along the promenade, in an old temple dedicated to the Goddess of the Sea. The small, intimate space was crammed with people on what appeared to be a festival day, given the copious offerings of fresh fruit and a roast pig's head that were laid out just inside the entrance. Further in, tubs of sand held dozens of flaring candles from which worshippers lit their joss sticks and approached the shrine on the back wall. Impressed by the atmosphere but soon in need of fresh air, we emerged from the dark, smoky interior to the bright sunshine on Stanley promenade.

A couple of dollars got us back from Stanley on the bus and we paid the one-dollar premium to ride on the upper deck of the *Silver Star* ferry across to Kowloon, needing to return in time for the sailaway that afternoon. Having learnt a painful lesson in Beijing, we made sure we did our souvenir shopping a very short walk from the ship at least an hour before the all-aboard deadline, buying a modestly priced silk cushion cover and silk wall hanging from an arts and crafts store. The store also catered for tourists with real money to burn (not us, obviously), selling jade, porcelain, wood carvings and paintings, at prices up to $US 150,000.

At the sailaway, a loudspeaker commentary from the bridge recounted the sad fate of *Queen Mary*'s sister ship *Queen Elizabeth*. After transporting American troops across the Atlantic during World War II and then many thousands of passengers over the decades to follow, the liner was eventually sold to a Hong Kong businessman, but in 1972 she mysteriously caught fire in Victoria Harbour. The half-submerged wreck later featured in the James Bond movie *The Man with the Golden Gun*. Finally, in the late 1990s, *Queen Elizabeth*'s remains were buried under land reclaimed for a new container terminal just a mile or so along the shore from where the *Amsterdam* was casting off.

We headed east out of Victoria Harbour as the setting sun lit up the dense ranks of skyscrapers lining the shore – and one small fishing village on stilts that had somehow escaped the march of progress.

At sea next day, a display of handmade blankets appeared in one of the public rooms. These had been knitted or crocheted by passengers during the voyage in aid of the Linus Project, a nationwide US charity donating blankets and soft toys to children in hospital. HAL had supplied the materials. At this stage, over one hundred of these wonderful pieces of work were on display, and many more were expected by the end of the cruise. On another sea day – when conditions allowed – there was a 5k fundraising walk around the deck, a tradition that HAL maintains across its entire fleet (5 kms = 3 miles = 10 laps). Passengers were invited to participate or just donate, with proceeds going to various cancer charities in the USA, Canada, UK, Australia, and Holland. In 2022, the donations went to a charity providing medical supplies to Ukraine.

Meanwhile, a flyer announced a passenger photo competition. Subject categories included landscape, urban, people, and abstract, and all entries would be printed and displayed in the photo gallery for fellow passengers to vote on. Winners would be revealed before arrival in Sydney. I began sorting through the hundreds of photos I'd already taken.

• **Mrs V:** I thought this one was a dead cert.

VIETNAM: Nha Trang

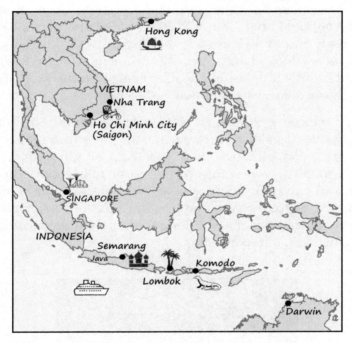

Set against a symphony of noise... my street was a stage for an anarchic dance of buses, trucks, cars, bicycles, cyclos, and motorbikes... It looked like the death-defying circus act of a trapeze family that, with each progressive trick, moved closer to disaster... I knew that, eventually, someone would miss, and a fractional miscalculation of speed or distance would leave some sad soul sprawled and bloody in the middle of the street.

(Dana Sachs, *The House on Dream Street – Memoir of an American Woman in Vietnam*)

The first of our two stops in Vietnam – Nha Trang, in the south east – was a brief one, since we needed to be back on board by 2:30. As the *Amsterdam* began its slow approach, the view along the seashore was of wooden huts on spindly stilts with more conventional brick houses stacked up behind, and steep, densely forested ridges as a backdrop. Right in front of us as we looked out from the promenade deck was a fleet of little blue fishing boats. Then, around a headland to the next bay, was the town and its long sandy beach.

A welcome party of sorts was gathering on the quayside. It's always nice when your hosts turn up early to greet you, although these seemed a bit glum (as well you might if you were greeting your fourteenth cruise ship in a week). There was a 'Welcome to Nha Trang' banner, a group of immigration officials, and six elegant ladies in traditional *ao dai* (long tunics), a splash of colour on this grey, damp morning.

A temporary open-air market was also being set up, ideal for last-minute souvenirs before re-boarding, or for any passengers unable or unwilling to go further ashore.

We were happy just to wander and see what happened, the only plan being to meet our Aussie friends for a swim later. Declining offers of taxis and rickshaws, we took our lives in our hands and walked towards the centre amid the noise and chaos on the streets. Hundreds of mopeds and bicycles were criss-crossing at busy intersections without colliding, but we couldn't see how we could cross ourselves, until we copied others and got the hang of just drifting over and letting the traffic glide around us.

It was hot, it was humid, and we had made the terrible mistake of leaving the ship before our morning coffee. As we walked along it became ominously clear that there weren't any coffee shops.

- **Mrs Verne:** The town's indoor market offered some respite from the heat and I distracted myself from thoughts of coffee by buying a scarf, ruthlessly beating the vendor down from ten to nine dollars. Then another trader offered the same scarf for three dollars as we walked away. I was happy enough to contribute to the local economy, though (OK, I admit it, we're just totally inept hagglers).

Some coffee shops finally turned up but we were distraught to find as we eagerly entered that they only sold packs of beans. We hailed a taxi to take us to the seafront, where we knew there were cafés, for our increasingly urgent fix.

- **Mrs V again:** But drinking the coffee turned out not to be so simple: there was a cup with little tin filter on top, but only the minutest amount of water to pour through it, which we did – assuming this was how they liked it in Vietnam – then tried to drink the resulting acrid, mouth puckering mud, our faces and stomachs creasing in agony. Fortunately a fellow tourist at a nearby table, noticing our predicament, explained that you were supposed to ask the waitress for extra water. We did, and finally got the coffee to taste just agreeably strong, with a hint of vanilla. Not bad for 36,000 dong ($US 1.50).

A taxi driver recommended visiting the town's pagoda where there was a giant white Buddha. Yet another temple, we thought, but we were swayed by the idea of a giant Buddha and, well, there wasn't a lot else to see in Nha Trang. Inside the pagoda, we removed our shoes as required, I lit a stick of incense but at the wrong end, we listened to the guide, had to pay a 'donation' to get our shoes back, and then were persuaded to 'donate' some more for postcards we didn't actually want. A fellow passenger later said he only gave a tenth of what we had given and the guide had seemed happy. But, we reasoned yet again, the temple and its people probably needed these few dollars more than we did.

Rain forced us to abandon our planned dip in the sea in favour of a nice lunch at a hotel near the beach. Having heard good things of Vietnamese food we tucked into spring rolls, chicken in ginger, and tuna, washed down with a cool beer. Outside, sheltering from a heavy shower, we asked a taxi driver about a long red banner strung across the road and he translated it roughly as

'Uncle Ho is great and will live in our hearts always.' We were to find out more about Uncle Ho at our next port of call, Ho Chi Minh City.

Bamboo is big in Vietnam: Nha Trang has a Golden Bamboo restaurant, a Miss Bamboo café and a Bamboo spa. An airline is called Bamboo Airways. Back at the dock, our last-minute souvenirs just had to be a bamboo bookmark for my collection and a silk cushion cover with a bamboo design.

So, a brief but representative introduction to Vietnam, as fleetingly seen by tourists: steamy weather, mopeds and rickshaws, market, temple, excellent food, and bamboo souvenirs.

Nha Trang was just a morning: we did what we could and enjoyed it, coming away with a few photos and some superficial impressions. It was the kind of place that a travel writer or blogger visits for a short while, describes vividly, then moves on – as in the words of author Paul Theroux:

This generalizing – the snap judgment of the traveler – is the reason travel writing can seem so crisp, so insightful to the reader, and so maddening to the person who knows the place well, or who inhabits the area, who does not recognize his or her home from the brisk description of the wisecracking wayfarer.

(*Deep South*)

Theroux was making a serious point, but in *The Happy Isles of Oceania* he has good fun with the stereotype of a tourist who flits around the world without really knowing where he has been. A man next to him on the plane to Auckland boasts that he has been all over the Pacific, including Fuji and Haiti, and that he and his wife are members of the Century Club, which you can only join if you have been to a hundred countries. 'What does "been to" mean?' muses Theroux. 'Pass through the airport? Spend a night? Get diarrhea there?'

In his account of a road trip around the US (*Blue Highways*), William Least Heat-Moon makes a similar point but takes it further, lamenting the tendency to sanitise and homogenise places in order to cater for here-today-gone-tomorrow tourists and to attract even more of them. He visits an old, overgrown fort in Georgia recently acquired by the National Park Service and earmarked for development. The park ranger tells him that if he were in charge he wouldn't change a thing, he loves the place too much:

But one day we'll have pavement so high-heeled ladies and overweight men can tiptoe a few steps to the Star Fort, see something they don't understand, take a snapshot of themselves, and hurry on. Without trees and isolation, you lose the mystery.

Lonely Planet once published a quiz to help you identify what kind of traveller you are and to guide you to the right cruise. Questions included:

1. Your top to-do destination is:
A. Jamaica   B. The Galápagos
C. Moorea

2. Your favourite food is:
A. a cheeseburger   B. soup and salad
C. freshly made ceviche

3. Your most likely souvenir would be:
A. jewellery   B. photos, alcohol
C. I take only memories and leave only footprints

4. You get an adrenaline rush:
A. on an escalator   B. on a water slide
C. scuba diving

5. You never go out without:
A. your phone   B. a snack
C. a smile

and so on...

And the results:

Mostly As: You love megaships with all the bells and whistles. You can breeze through the Caribbean without ever having to disembark in a port.

Mostly Bs: It's about the people, the culture, and nature, but you want a comfy pillow at the end of the day.

Mostly Cs: Adventure is your middle name. You're looking for something unconventional, authentic and highly personalised.

So, which are you? Which were we? I'm not entirely sure. Probably in the Bs. Mrs Verne does not like being uncomfortable.

When sociologist Arthur Berger and his wife went on a cruise for the first time he could not resist studying his fellow passengers, and later wrote it all up in an academic paper. Being on a cruise for some people, he said, is like a regression to an ideal childhood, where free food is brought on demand and we receive unconditional love from staff who are trained to be friendly and accommodating to our needs. Regression helps us deal with the anxieties and disappointments of everyday life, which may also explain why many feel compelled to take multiple cruises. 'We are, psychologically, back in the Garden of Eden.'

Ho Chi Minh City (Saigon)

The trusty *Amsterdam* continued on down through the South China Sea, and next morning we docked at Phu My, a two-hour drive from Ho Chi Minh City. On one side of the estuary was a sprawling container port and some heavy industry, on the other, mangrove swamps. Not much to see here, but we had booked seats on the shuttle bus to Ho Chi Minh City at $US 59 each. A full-blown HAL tour of the city would have cost $149 per person. (A general rule of thumb for shore excursions is that the revenue is split between the cruise line, a middleman agency, and the actual tour provider, so the customer may expect 149 dollars' worth of value but the tour guide only receives 50 dollars. And if there's a problem, the customer usually blames the guide.) My back was still stiff and painful, so on the shuttle bus I had to stand up every few minutes to ease the muscles. I felt a bit of an idiot, but my fellow passengers were probably mature enough themselves to guess what the deal was.

Ho Chi Minh City – formerly Saigon until 1976 and still commonly called that by many Vietnamese – is known as the Pearl of the Orient, a title also claimed by Hong Kong, Shanghai, the Philippines, and a Chinese restaurant near you. Our drop-off point in the centre was the Rex Hotel, famous as a watering hole for US officers and journalists during the Vietnam War but now a five-star luxury establishment on a wide, tree-lined boulevard. In a square opposite was a statue of the man himself, communist revolutionary Ho Chi Minh. In stifling heat, our sightseeing began at the Reunification (ex-President's) Palace; we had to agree with the Rough Guide description of it as 'a whitewashed concrete edifice with all the charm of a municipal library', although we were unable to check out the interior as this major attraction was closed for lunch. We did inspect the famous gates that were stormed by North Vietnamese tanks in 1975 just before the fall of Saigon, and they were intact, doing a great job of keeping the tourists out. After a lunch of *pho* – noodles and beef strips – in an air-conditioned mall, we headed off to the War Remnants Museum, probably the site most frequented by visitors to Vietnam.

Inside the perimeter was quite a collection of well-preserved American military hardware – tanks, artillery, aircraft – and some visitors were excitedly taking selfies in front of the big Chinook helicopter and a cool fighter jet. Entering the museum building we were greeted by elegant, smiling ladies in beautiful silk tunics and ushered towards the first room, which was about the 1960s protest movement against the Vietnam War.

Further along were glass cabinets full of various guns and ammunition, all labelled factually and without comment.

But on the next floor came the really shocking material – graphic photos of the war's victims. Two whole rooms were dedicated to chemical defoliant Agent Orange and its horrific effects, both at the time and on later generations; another, to the large number of casualties from landmines since the war. This was the opposite of snap-it-and-go tourism, and not the place for Theroux's 'wisecracking wayfarers'. You don't just breeze through the War Remnants Museum.

On the top floor, though, a change of tone: a before-and-after exhibition, grainy black and white photos of bomb-damaged sites next to recent colour photos of the same places, now rebuilt. And there we came to the end of our visit. Yes, presentation had been one-sided, but it was hard to dispute the basic message that the Communist Party was thrusting in our faces: Vietnam had prevailed in the face of a terrible war and was now united, peaceful, and prosperous.

Despite the history of colonialism and war, Vietnamese people seemed welcoming to all comers. Unfortunately for them, Vietnam is a one-party state without freedom of speech, assembly or religion, where dissidents are locked up, often for years. That does not seem to stop Western democracies enthusiastically setting up trade links with the regime, though. In 2015 Newhaven town council in the UK launched a short-lived design competition for a tribute to Ho Chi Minh who, it was a little surprising to learn, once worked as a pastry chef on the Newhaven-Dieppe ferry after the First World War. 'Fury at council's statue of commie tyrant' reported one

British tabloid, while *The Huffington Post* went with 'Before Ho Chi Minh Became A Mass Murderer He Was Known For His Pastries'. Although the idea was then dropped, the council were happy to receive the Vietnamese ambassador and pay their respects to the 'revered' Ho Chi Minh in the hope of selling more stuff to his compatriots.

The other must-see for visitors to Ho Chi Minh City are the nearby Cu Chi Tunnels, a vast underground network used by Viet Cong soldiers during the war but now limited to a couple of stretches specially widened to accommodate Western body types. Tripadvisor invites you to 'pose for photos peeking out of a camouflaged trapdoor, climb aboard an old American army tank, or visit the shooting range'. You can tell how popular the tunnels are from the many photos of smiling tourists posted online, and reviews praising the guides as knowledgeable but also as 'very funny' and 'a good laugh'. We weren't sure what to think – surely those tunnels used to be a matter of life and death? But there was no time left for more sightseeing, or for a cold beer at the tastefully named Apocalypse Now, a bar in the city that boasts an 'international crowd going wild to pounding techno music'. Apparently the place really takes off after midnight, but that was way past our bedtime, and in any case the *Amsterdam* was calling.

At the Mekong Delta rest area on the way back to the ship, a group of us enjoyed delicious Vietnamese ice cream and grumbled about the short amount of time we'd had for visiting Ho Chi Minh City. As we later told the shore excursions staff, a second day here instead of Nha Trang would have been preferable. To be fair to Holland America, our itinerary on this cruise was actually quite generous compared to most, with two-day stops in Yokohama, Kobe, Tianjin, Shanghai and Hong Kong so far, and another due at Singapore – our next port of call.

Holland America is pretty good at laying on themed evenings and events for sea days, and the amount of effort it puts into decorating the restaurant and dressing the staff is impressive. Each event costs the cruise line thousands of dollars. By now we'd enjoyed a Black and Gold Ball, Movie Star Night, Kimono Night, an Oriental High Tea, and an Oriental Evening where the dining room was decked out in red Chinese lanterns and our waiters wore silk shirts and hats (as did quite a few diners). About two months in advance of a cruise, HAL sends out a calendar of all scheduled theme nights to give everyone the chance to pack their fancy dress and party paraphernalia, which for some requires an entire extra suitcase. Maybe we didn't get the memo, but we totally failed to pack anything gold, silver, movie-related, Chinese, or Halloweeny, with one exception: we had kimonos (or rather, simplified easy-to-wear versions called yukata that we use as dressing gowns), and so on Kimono Night, for once, we were more dressed up than our dinner companions.

A feature of HAL Grand Voyages (and no doubt on other shipping lines), whether you're on all the way or just for a segment, is the 'pillow gift': on some formal evenings you will return to your cabin to find a small present on the bed with a note of appreciation from the management. Ours included a travel bag embossed with *Grand Asia and Australia Voyage*, a leather-bound journal, and a bookmark-shaped magnifying glass. Now if it had been a magnifying glass-shaped bookmark...

SINGAPORE

My uncle, a gentle soul, once poured a bowl of rice pudding all over my aunt because he and two army mates had each sworn an oath to do that to the first person who served them rice after the war. Now, in Singapore, I hoped to find out more.

Nagasaki, Saigon, Singapore. We had not set out to visit places associated with death and destruction – also known as 'dark tourism' – but now it seemed that we were doing it anyway. It would be odd to go to Nagasaki or Saigon and not bump up against the dark events in their history, but Singapore, not so much: in this vibrant city with so many other distractions, you would have to find your way out to a distant suburb near the airport to do as we did and visit a museum relating to World War Two. Why did we do this? Because my uncle was a prisoner of war in a Japanese concentration camp in that suburb, Changi. It was not something he talked about when we used to stay with them in Kent every Christmas.

For the second time in three days we found ourselves surveying the hell of war. A tour group from our ship was there too, quietly taking in the moving testimonies of captives and the displays of personal items. Frank descriptions of the appalling treatment of prisoners were balanced by tales of inmate resourcefulness and mutual kindness that helped to keep up morale.

My uncle was lucky not to have been killed in 1942, when the Japanese overran the hospital where he worked and bayoneted many of the staff and patients;

then, as a prisoner, lucky not to be chosen to work on the Burma-Thailand 'Death' Railway, which cost thousands of lives. He survived, despite the hard labour, beatings, deaths from tropical disease and a near-starvation diet of mainly boiled rice. He weighed only six stone (84 pounds, or 38 kg) on his eventual return home in 1945. In the years that I knew him Uncle Steve was always a bit deaf, but as his daughter later explained, his hearing had probably been damaged by the torture technique of a gunshot next to the head. To this day, she still wears a ring he made in the camp from a silver Japanese coin.

So, when my aunt served up that rice pudding for the first time since the war, Uncle Steve felt honour bound to tip it over her, although I am told that he immediately apologised and rushed to clean her up. He had kept the promise to his two mates – we don't know if they ever did the same.

I could just mention here that our first day in Singapore was also my birthday; Mrs V forgot it, having lost track of all dates during the cruise, as it's easy to do (she said).

> • **Mrs Verne again:** I did forget, but <u>he</u> never, ever will.

After our harrowing museum visit, a very Singaporean lunch of chicken satay, fried rice with an egg on top, poppadom and a Tiger Beer set us up for an afternoon of sightseeing. At Raffles Hotel we were greeted by a Sikh doorman looking splendid in his immaculate white uniform and turban (a Raffles tradition, also available in the gift shop in the form of a soft toy). Our main aim was to visit the Long Bar and try a gin-based cocktail for which it is famous: the Singapore Sling. The gin comes from a London distillery owned by a descendant of Sir Stamford Raffles, the founder of colonial Singapore, and contains some ingredients from the Malay Peninsula such as pomelo peel, lemongrass, and jasmine flowers. The subtlety of the gin was lost on us, however, as we thirstily knocked back about half a pint of the fruity pink liquid, a refreshing mix of sweet and citrus flavours with only a moderate hit of alcohol. The recipe for the Sling was on display in the bar, the liquid ingredients all in 'jiggers', an old British measurement for a sailor's daily rum ration (one jigger = 1.5oz, or 45ml). Great word.

> one and a half jiggers gin
> half jigger cherry brandy
> 1 dash Benedictine
> 1 dash Cointreau
> 1 drop bitters
> 3 jiggers pineapple juice (or to taste)
> quarter jigger grenadine syrup
> half jigger fresh lemon or lime juice
>
> Garnish with a slice of pineapple and a cherry.

A Singapore Sling in the old-world elegance of Raffles' shaded Palm Court is definitely recommended. Staying here is another matter: a night in the Rudyard Kipling Suite, with butler service, will set you back about 1500 US dollars. The writer did stay here in the 1880s and praised the hotel's food, which Raffles has proudly quoted in their advertising ever since. Well, Kipling certainly said 'Feed at Raffles', but what they conveniently leave out is the rest of what he wrote, no doubt grumpy from the heat and humidity: 'Raffles Hotel, where the food is as excellent as the rooms are bad. Let the traveller take note. Feed at Raffles and sleep at the Hotel de l'Europe.' More recently, while boosting Singapore as the best city in the world, a CNN Travel feature tried to evoke a British ambience for the hotel but got it hilariously wrong: 'Perfect place to workshop your veddy Bwiddish accent' (who's that supposed to be – Elmer Fudd?) and 'Today it remains as posh as Victoria Beckham'. So, not posh at all, then.

The legacy of colonialism in the city was still very visible in street names – Queen Street, Victoria Street, Empress Place, King George's Avenue – while Raffles was everywhere, his name on scores of schools, hospitals, shopping centres, restaurants and streets. Elsewhere in the world, statues of controversial historical figures were being torn down, but here a bronze statue of him was still standing. At the time of our visit, Raffles' reputation was apparently intact as a kind of benevolent imperialist who in the 1820s had commissioned a town plan and set up a free port, a school for the sons of local chiefs and the first magistrates court. He also abolished gambling, cock-fighting and slavery.

Of course, Singapore is now a shiny modern metropolis looking to the future, not the past. But next we headed for a less glitzy side of the city.

We once planned an amazing no-fly trip to India. It would have broken with our habit of linking up several cruises, but the result would have been just as adventurous: sailing from the UK with Holland America, then disembarking at Cochin in India's south and spending five weeks touring the country while the ship continued on to Indonesia. We would then have reboarded the same ship in Mumbai on its return journey to the UK.

I spent weeks doing research. An Indrail pass could get us around, but would we be comfortable, given that we find it difficult to sleep on trains? And what about the heat, and the food? Where trains were not available, going by car would be easy because rental companies supply vehicles with drivers (who actually sleep in the car if it's a long trip). In the south we could tour tea and spice plantations, cruise backwaters on a houseboat or visit hill stations, and way up north in the Golden Triangle of Delhi, Agra and Jaipur we'd see medieval forts, marvel at the Taj Mahal, ride an elephant, and shop for amazing souvenirs in colourful bazaars (do they sell bookmarks in India?). Our imaginations were fired up, and we were getting that familiar urge to quickly pay the deposit before we lost out on a good cabin. First, though, we had to apply via HAL for permission to disembark and reboard weeks later at a different port. We had been allowed to do this in the past for other countries, so did not anticipate any problems.

After a tense wait, we heard that the Indian authorities had rejected our request, without explanation. But, within weeks of this disappointment came the wonderful news that our first grandchild was on the way in America where our son lived, and we gladly put all our energies (and cruise money) into a new plan: getting to Baltimore in time for the birth in May, though still by ship, naturally. There were no direct transatlantic crossings scheduled for April, but a three-week cruise on P&O's *Oriana* could take us from Southampton to Charleston via Madeira, St Maarten, Jamaica, Mexico, Key West, New Orleans and Port Canaveral. We booked it. Our arrival in Baltimore would be at the end of April, about three days before the due date. All our daughter-in-law had to do was hold the baby in until we got there.

This was not our first cruise with P&O: on a previous trip we had sailed from Barbados back to Southampton on the *Azura,* a big white tower block of a vessel with a capacity of 3,500 passengers, whereas the *Oriana* was about half that, neither too large nor too small. Once on board, we found our cabin to be spacious and comfortable. Restaurant food was generally good, and we liked the 'Freedom Dining' option – flexible mealtimes, sit where you're told to – which meant interesting new dinner companions each evening.

So, instead of tea plantations, elephant rides and the Taj Mahal, we had Caribbean beaches, French Quarter jambalaya and jazz, and a double helping of the world's best key lime pie. The imminent arrival of our first grandchild was on our minds throughout, of course. Would we make it in time? In fact, the birth was late and we made it to Baltimore with a week to spare. Had we gone to India we would have missed meeting our new grandson within hours of his birth; instead, we were able to stay in the US for a couple of months on proud babysitting duty. Our India plans were filed away in the hope that we could dust them off at some future date.

But now, in Singapore, we had a few hours in which to experience *Little* India.

Using our two-day bus/rail pass we took an underground train to the Little India station. We emerged into a different world: to our surprise, the Hindu Festival of Deepavali, aka Diwali, was in full swing, with countless banners strung across the street depicting a lit candle – the festival celebrates the triumph of light over darkness – flanked by 'Happy Deepavali' messages in English and Tamil.

Wandering into a temporary covered market we were met by a riot of colour: long strings of glittering baubles and miniature bells, huge lanterns, shiny silk saris, flower garlands, and thousands of soft toy elephants. Porcelain statues of Hindu gods, too, especially the elephant-headed Ganesh, bringer of good luck. This was a real festival for locals, not a show laid on for foreigners. The narrow aisles were full of people strolling, stopping, pointing, buying; we struggled to get through the crush.

Escaping the heat and hubbub of the market, we retraced our steps. Things were pretty busy around the nearby Sri Veeramakaliamman Temple, its façade a magnificent tower of carved goddesses, warriors, assorted musicians, cherubs, and lions.

The goddesses may in fact have been just the one, Kali, appearing in her many guises. Inside the entrance was a place to put your shoes, and a rack of little bells to announce your arrival. In the main hall a few worshippers sat on the floor or prostrated themselves, while others lined up for a priest to quickly dab some paste on their forehead with his thumb. Two statues off the hall showed a more ferocious side of Kali: one wearing a necklace of human skulls, the other feasting on the entrails of a queen who had wanted to kill her own newborn baby (it's a long story). Outside the temple a poster advertised a forthcoming week of prayer which, we later found, meant a marathon of chanting from a sacred text, supposed to bring better health and 'protection from evil forces and government agencies'.

Having always imagined reincarnation to be short and painless – maybe a waiting room, a judgment from on high, and back you go – I was surprised to learn that Hindu and Buddhist sinners have to pass through hell before being allowed to return. As in Dante's *Inferno*, this hell has a series of circles where punishments are matched to sins and repeat, over and over, until eventually the sinner can leave and be reincarnated in a lower form. Today we'd had two glimpses of hell: one very real at Changi, this other one – who knows?

Back at the cruise terminal we continued the afternoon's theme with an Indian meal in the food court, reflecting that Little India had been gripping and colourful but hot, humid, and very crowded. Our legs were aching and we were desperate for a lie-down in an air-conditioned cabin.

Perhaps we no longer needed to see the real thing after all?

Our second day in Singapore was just a morning, all-aboard time being 2pm even though the ship's departure would not be until 4pm. There were complaints from some passengers, but perhaps the Captain did not want a repeat of that little spot of trouble in Tianjin. In the humid 90-degree (32C) heat of late October, we strolled around Singapore's beautiful Botanic Gardens, which has a famous orchid collection. Mrs V bought me a handmade pressed flower bookmark as a belated birthday gift.

• **Mrs Verne here:** After a lot of heavy hints.

We made sure not to drop anything anywhere: Singapore's laws on personal behaviour and cleanliness are notoriously strict. Fines are meted out for littering or spitting, chewing gum is completely banned, and even hugging a stranger is illegal (I quite approve of that one). More serious crimes merit a caning and prison. Females are not allowed to be caned in Singapore, but they are in neighbouring Indonesia, as long the caners themselves are also female. The *Straits Times* in 2019 ran the headline 'Indonesia unveils new female flogging squad', reporting that a new recruit had just done her first flogging, of a woman caught in a hotel room with a man. The newbie flogger was initially reticent, but persevered. 'I think she did a good job. Her technique was nice,' said the police chief approvingly.

Our next stop on this cruise? Indonesia.

INDONESIA

Steaming south from Singapore, we soon crossed the Equator but chose not to attend the usual shenanigans with King Neptune condemning crew members to kissing a fish, being covered in gunk and then thrown into the swimming pool. We had already seen this ritual twice during our cruise around South America, so it was no longer a novelty. The Crossing the Line ceremony has a long tradition: in the 18th century victims were ducked in the ocean while under sail, which surprisingly did not always end well, and in the next century even Charles Darwin was forced to undergo a disagreeable 'watery ordeal' on *HMS Beagle* – blindfolded, slathered with pitch and paint and then ducked in a large bath. In the 1950s Sir Harold Nicolson, a British diplomat with a dry wit and a love of the classics, claimed not to have enjoyed watching the ceremony on a cruise to Java with his wife Vita because the great Neptune was treated as a comic character:

And here he was... striding up to the forward end of the bathing pool, wearing a long flaxen wig and a long flaxen beard, under which I detected the fine features of the games-instructor... V, owing to her Spanish blood, was much amused. And I, not wishing to be an outsider, smiled with the utmost benevolence.

(*Journey to Java*)

But Nicolson and his wife had a brilliant idea about the Equator itself: wouldn't it be nice if the line could be marked by a row of buoys encircling the globe so that you would know exactly when you crossed it? (I *think* this was a joke.)

We couldn't avoid the Neptune theme completely, however. That evening the dining room was awash with sea-related decorations: fish streamers, balloons in the shape of turtles, octopus and fish, stewards wearing fishy hats. At the Gala Ball our cruise director and hostess sat on thrones, dressed as Neptune and a mermaid, while the band played *Yellow Submarine*. Of course.

En route to Semarang, somewhere off the starboard side will have been the volcanic island of Krakatoa, which is west of Java. Everyone says the 1968 disaster movie *Krakatoa: East of Java* got it wrong, but not if you go the long way round, surely?

- **Mrs V:** That's a very old joke, you know.

Semarang, Java

As we drew into the beautiful harbour, ships of all nations lay anchored around us... A picturesque corps of native dancers were performing on the quay with prodigious energy. A band played. 'I wonder what the tune is?' said a passenger. 'They are playing The Dollars Are Coming,' I replied.

(Cecil Roberts, *The Grand Cruise*)

At the quayside in Semarang, passengers lined the promenade deck to watch the performance below. A formation of male dancers was padding back and forth, resplendent in colourful costumes, feathered head-dresses and face paint much like traditional Native

Americans. Ankle bells jingled to the rhythm of their stomping feet. By contrast, a figure in a bright yellow tiger costume was doing its own thing, a freewheeling solo away from the main group. Music was by a gamelan ensemble of xylophones, drums, gongs, and two singers.

To the side, awaiting their turn to perform, sat these exquisite ladies.

The cynical Cecil Roberts quote above could apply to many cruise ports around the world that are heavily reliant on tourism but not, I think, to Semarang, despite the energetic dancers and band. This is partly because the area has little tourist infrastructure anyway (other than one famous attraction, Borobudur), but also because Holland America has family connections with Indonesia, recruiting many crew members locally and training them at its own school in Jakarta. When its ships visit Indonesia, as they often do, something unusual happens: while passengers go ashore, up to a thousand friends and family members of the crew are welcomed aboard for the day. As some of the crew may not have been home in perhaps nine months, this must be an exciting and emotional day for them. On reflection, I suspect that the dancers and musicians on the quayside may have been welcoming the crew rather than us and our dollars.

An excursion to the Borobudur temple complex in the interior of Java was an option, and judging from the convoy of buses leaving the dock quite a few passengers had signed up. At $US 200 per person and travel time of three hours each way, this was not for us. We soon learned from taxi drivers that the few alternatives were themselves two hours distant, and having heard about heavy traffic and the poor state of roads we could not risk it. Instead, a visit to the old Dutch quarter for a cup of Java coffee seemed a good start. The road into town was indeed in terrible shape, with flooded areas either side and obvious signs of poverty. We briefly checked out a colonial Dutch church, a handsome white building with a light and airy interior, but to our European eyes unremarkable, except for an impressive organ and the oddity of rattan seats instead of wooden pews. It was mostly empty that Sunday morning, probably between services. To our dismay, the café opposite the church did not sell coffee. I wanted to explore the old town, but Mrs V – needing caffeine, *now* – was reluctant to walk around this rather run-down area, breathing in traffic fumes and wilting in steamy 90-degree heat. Crossing the Equator did not mean we had immediately jumped ahead to balmy spring weather. The solution: a taxi to a modern shopping mall, armed with half a million rupiah.

Here, you could buy some very special coffee. Not the standard stuff we actually ordered, but a brew new to us: kopi luwak, 'a very rare coffee that has been digested by luwak'. Our Aussie friends Paul and Karen, who had also found their way to the mall, explained how this coffee was made and why it was banned in Australia. Luwaks (civets, which are cat-like) are fed a diet of coffee 'cherries', but they can only digest the outer skin while the beans pass straight through, acquiring an interesting new aroma and flavour along the way. Marketing hype usually refers to it as the most expensive coffee in the world (rather than calling it, say, 'cat poo coffee'); in Semarang it cost about eight dollars, but it seems in the US a cup can sell for up to ten times that. According to retired customs official Paul, Australia bans luwak coffee because of health concerns (can't imagine why), although animal cruelty and fakery are other reasons to avoid the drink. Should you need one.

Killing time in the mall, I noticed a store called The Athlete's Foot. Who would name their footwear company after a fungal infection, I wondered, but it turns out they have been trading for decades and own a number of stores around the world. By early afternoon we decided to call it a day, heading off to catch the shuttle bus back to the ship. First, though, we had to run the gauntlet of some very forward street vendors lined up next to the bus, finally emerging unscathed but with a leather bookmark, a traditional wooden *wayang* puppet and a patchwork quilt cover to use up the rest of our fifty dollars' worth of rupiah.

'Hullo, yes, you sir. Good morning,' he cried. 'You wanta one nice woman.'

I said, no, not quite as early in the day as that.

'Well then, you wanta see Pompeian dances... All-a-girls naked. Vair artistic, vair smutty, vair French.'

I still said no, and he went on to suggest other diversions rarely associated with Sunday morning.

(Evelyn Waugh, *Labels*)

Our experience of touts and street sellers in East Asia had been pretty good, and they were certainly less aggressive than in other parts of the world where we would be pestered with offers of a taxi, a tour, a souvenir or a discount at a jewellery store, and often all of these at once, multiple times. Never 'artistic' girls, though, possibly due to the presence of my lovely wife.

American literary critic and keen traveller Paul Fussell was pestered so badly on his wanderings that in Haiti he even hired a tout to fend off the others (or so he says). They are a greater threat than sharks, fetid water and appalling food, he claimed in *Abroad*, and one particular nationality is most at risk:

Americans seem their favorite targets, not just because of their careless ways with money and their instinctive generosity but also their non-European innocence about the viler dimensions of human nature and their desire to be liked, their impulse to say 'Good morning' back instead of 'Go away'. It's a rare American who, asked 'Where you from, Sir?' will venture 'Screw you' instead of 'Boise'.

Fussell invented a new category of visitor: the anti-tourist. Neither snobbish traveller nor package tourist, the anti-tourist combines the two. He tries to blend in by not carrying a camera and by speaking the language, even if badly. Staying in unlikely hotels is another trick, though risky, as is using public transportation ('the more complicated and confusing the better... which may end with the anti-tourist stranded miles out of town, cold and alone on the last tram of the night'). The most popular way to avoid looking like a tourist, he concludes, is to lounge at a café table and 'with palpable contempt scrutinize the passing sheep'. If addressed by a lonely tourist, mutter 'Je ne parle pas anglais', look at your watch, and leave.

Does any of this sound familiar? It does to me – I often hide my camera, try to speak the language (not possible in Asia), ride my luck on buses, and feel slightly superior when watching passing tourists from a prime café spot. It doesn't fool anyone, obviously.

As for the ship's excursion to Borobudur, we saw the bus convoy return later behind the sirens and flashing lights of a police escort, which apparently had cleared the way through dense traffic to ensure the tour groups arrived back in time. The consensus of those on the tour was that, amazing though the 9th-century temple ruins were, it had been such a *long* day and they were so *very* tired.

Lombok

Lombok Island: east of Java (no really, it is). More music and colour on the quayside here but on a smaller scale, as we shuffled past a line of young men in traditional batik sarongs and gold silk shirts, each with a pair of cymbals that they clanged in unison to greet us. As usual on this cruise it was all very dignified, unlike in the Caribbean, where crew members dress up as, say, pirates and stand near the gangway, urging passengers to pose for a holiday snap. We've never been tempted, though I do enjoy checking out the setup before anyone goes ashore, when you're likely to look down from the promenade deck and see the photographer chatting to a six-foot-high crocodile. At least that's harmless: Princess Cruises got into trouble in New Zealand when some of their Filipino crew donned fake grass skirts and drew black marks on their faces to perform a Maori welcome ceremony, causing understandable offence.

With another shortish day in port, our aims were modest – to see a bit of the island and maybe find a nice beach. But not on a ship's excursion. We hired a taxi to take us up the coast from the port of Lembar, and at last got a taste of rural Asia after the recent string of cities on the *Amsterdam*'s itinerary. We passed corn fields, rice paddies and small vegetable plots, while the roadside was dotted with flowers in bloom and clusters of palm trees, above which came the occasional glimpse of a mosque's powder-blue dome.

Horse-drawn carts were everywhere and, especially later on when school had ended for the day, hundreds of motor scooters. Poverty was more evident as we sailed through the villages, where uncollected rubbish clogged streams or piled up next to houses (Paul Theroux's definition of tourism was the mobile rich visiting the inert poor). From the coastal road we could see signs of a traditional fishing industry: in some of the bays large, rickety bamboo platforms stood like toy oil rigs with nets suspended from a frame, while outrigger canoes lined the beaches, their inverted V-shaped supports on either side eerily suggestive of giant spiders lying in wait.

Twenty miles north of Lembar we reached Senggigi and asked the driver to help us look for a suitable place to stop and relax. We rejected a couple but then seized on the Sheraton Beach Resort, an oasis of luxury compared to what we had just passed. First-World guilt prevented us from openly cheering at our find, but we simply wanted somewhere safe for a swim. On a shaded patio looking out onto immaculately tended tropical gardens, we sat back with some five-star coffee and pastries. Almost like being on a cruise ship. Then for the next hour or so we lounged on the beach and swam in the warm waters, me drowsily imagining that the outrigger canoes further round the bay might be scuttling along the sands towards us. Following a simple lunch at the open-air bar our driver picked us up and we headed back down the coast. After our luxurious morning we were glad (or feeling guilty enough) to agree to his inevitable suggestion of a stop at a little souvenir shop he just happened to know, where we bought a painted wooden gecko and a cotton bedspread with gecko motif. (Vietnam has its bamboo, Indonesia its gecko, although not as many as it used to have – catching them for use in traditional Chinese medicine is a good source of income).

Today we had been in full tourist mode – taxi, sun lounger on beach, familiar food in a Western-style hotel – but the next day promised to be more unusual: the island of Komodo. There be dragons.

Komodo Island

After leaving Lombok the ship continued east, and by the following morning we had reached the island of Komodo and anchored in a bay.

In bright sunshine we had a clear view of the scrubby, parched landscape and of a fishing village built on stilts as protection against roaming dragons. I was booked to join a walking tour at 11am.

Perhaps unwisely, I had already read up on the giant lizards. They grow to ten feet long and have razor-sharp claws and a venomous bite, so if their prey (mostly pigs and deer) manages to escape after an attack it then dies slowly from being poisoned. And they do sometimes attack humans: several people have been killed or injured in recent years, including a local boy and a Singaporean tourist. (The *Amsterdam*'s daily programme helpfully told us that a dragon could 'gobble down an adult in a matter of minutes'.) Their acute sense of smell can detect carrion or even just blood from miles away – menstruating female passengers are strongly advised not to go ashore. Komodo dragons live in trees for their first three years to avoid the adults, who have been known to snack on their young.

But I couldn't back out now. I boarded the tender with my fellow excursionists, of various ages and nationalities. (Mrs Verne had been too scared – 'sensible', she said – to go on the tour.) Temperature ashore: 100F, 38C. My group of about twenty was escorted by three rangers, each armed with a long pole as sole protection against any dragons that we might encounter.

That's right – no guns, just a forked stick. We nervously followed a dusty trail through the forest, spotting occasional deer and a boar before finally coming across several dragons lying around an almost dry water hole; alert, they moved their heads and watched us closely as we gawped from no more than about twenty feet away with nothing between us. Speaking quietly, our guide told us not to take flash photos or make sudden movements (as if); a previous tour group that morning had had to move on quickly when the dragons started showing too much interest in them. Slowly, hardly breathing, I took some photos and after a few minutes we cautiously edged away.

As we trekked further through the bush, an elderly American lady near me was beginning to lag behind in the heat and one of the guides had to help her along. I was torn – as a decent chap, do I also hang back and show concern, or catch up with the others for safety in numbers? True, there was a guide, but he was supporting the old lady and I no longer trusted him to spot danger and leap to our defence with his stick. I decided to stay with her, reasoning that I could always use her as a human shield while he battled the ravening beasts.

Fortunately, we reached the end of our walk without incident. En route we had passed a weak-looking deer with a bloody stump instead of an antler, obviously torn off by a dragon that was no doubt tracking the scent and would finish the poor animal off at its leisure.

Back at the beach, vendors were lined up under makeshift tarpaulin covers, selling mostly T-shirts and carved Komodo dragons of all sizes, including huge. I bought a very small one, made from hibiscus wood, while the vendor's wife stood there breastfeeding her baby. He offered to sell me some Indonesian pearls and said he'd pray for me. I declined, but later felt bad not buying more from this gentle man and his young family.

The *Amsterdam* set sail mid afternoon. It was then announced that our forthcoming visit to Port Moresby, Papua New Guinea, was being cancelled because of 'security concerns'. We had not researched the country and knew nothing about it, until our Australian friends explained that it had a dangerous reputation and expressed surprise that the port had been on the ship's itinerary in the first place. I discovered later that the hugely well-travelled Paul Theroux actually included Port Moresby on his list of the world's top ten dangerous locations:

> *One of the most dangerous, crime-ridden cities in the world, inhabited by drifters and squatters, locally known as 'rascals', and career criminals, many of whom, wearing woolly hats, come from the Highlands and are looking for prey.*

> (*The Tao of Travel*)

What was Holland America thinking? A couple of days later we read that Prince Charles (now King) and his wife Camilla were currently visiting Papua New Guinea, so maybe they didn't want any cruise riff-raff there at the same time. According to the UK press, Charles made a speech in the local Tok Pisin dialect, and he was known in the language as 'nambawan pikinini bilong Misis Kwin'.

What are your chances of being murdered on a cruise ship? Mrs V never walks the deck alone after dark, for fear of getting pushed overboard by a burly maniac emerging from the shadows.

Perhaps she's been reading too many cruise ship novels. Not romances, of course – not her thing – but murder mysteries. If you search for cruise-related books on Amazon you will find, apart of course from the excellent *Around the World in 80 Cruise Ships: How We*

Cruise Hopped the Globe Without Ever Setting Foot in an Airport, scores of novels in a particular genre: the Cruise Ship Cozy Mystery. The mystery will invariably relate to a murder, or multiple murders, solved in due course by an amateur sleuth who happens to be on board, and it will be 'cozy' because the violence tends to take place off stage and anything dubious or indelicate such as sex is not dwelt upon. The most prolific authors have published whole series of novels set on fictional ships, managing to conjure up murders even on, say, a cupcake-themed cruise, or between rival yoga groups. One author used to be part of a magic act, and now 'uses her insider knowledge' to write shipborne murder mysteries. What kind of inside knowledge would be useful for murder – sawing a body in half, making things disappear? If you're a pet lover you may prefer the sub-genre of Cruise Ship Cozy Animal Mystery: it's still the humans that get bumped off, but the sleuth has a clever feline sidekick on board with her (or a talking parrot, in the case of the magician's assistant).

The Cozy Mystery authors are mostly female, though you will find one or two men writing in a similar vein – one publishes a series of *Cruise Ship Crime Investigators* novels (cleverly echoing the name of America's long-running TV programme *CSI*). Murder is a theme here too, but the approach is less cosy and more muscular: instead of a middle-aged lady with a cat, a crack team of ex-special forces men are called in to investigate. The reality, as you may have guessed, is much less deadly than the fiction, for although a ship might seem an ideal opportunity for dumping someone overboard, passenger murder rates are actually extremely low, with only around fifteen killings in the last twenty years, worldwide.

- **Mrs Verne again:** I don't know why he's obsessing about murders when this is supposed to be a light and entertaining account of cruising to the other side of the world. Just the two of us in an enclosed space for three months. But never mind murders – why is it that when you ask for a table for two in a cruise restaurant, they seat you just a foot away from the next table? That's a mystery worth solving.

Slightly less rare than murder at sea is accidental drowning by falling overboard, or in the pool, or when a ship sinks (the only major cruise ship sinking in the 21st century so far has been the *Costa Concordia*, which claimed 32 lives). In times gone by, long sea voyages were so dangerous that drowning was always a possibility, as writer Samuel Johnson noted: 'being in a ship is being in a jail, with the chance of being drowned'. (Generally averse to seagoing anyway, he also said that a man in jail has more room, better food and better company – a good line to remember next time you need to complain about a cruise.) A century later, the risk was so well known that a schoolmaster in Dickens' *Hard Times* sets his pupil this statistical problem: '...in a given time a hundred thousand persons went to sea on long voyages, and only five hundred of them were drowned or burnt to death. What is the percentage?' So, 'only' one death in every 200 passengers was seen as a pretty good result in the 19th century, whereas today the probability of drowning on a cruise is really remote, more like one in several million.

If you are on one of those rare cruises where a serial killer is not on the loose, you may still be lucky to hear some other emergency announced over the tannoy in code, repeated three times. The not-so-secret codes include *Alpha* (medical emergency), *Bravo* (fire), *Charlie* (security threat), *Oscar* (man overboard), and *Zulu* (fight between passengers). During one of our recent *QM2* transatlantic crossings, not far from the coast of Nova Scotia, our Captain made the dramatic announcement – no codes, just plain English – that a medical evacuation by helicopter was imminent. To the crew he gave the curious order 'Hands to flying stations', but then banned all passengers from the open decks and even our own stateroom balconies. We could hear a great deal of laughter from the cabin next door as they went out onto their balcony over and over again to check for the helicopter.

Should a death occur on board, the body can be stored in the ship's morgue for up to a week, and most cruise ships can house three to six bodies. Until the 1970s, though, ships did not have a morgue and it was reportedly the practice to wrap a body and store it in the food freezer. Hence the old joke: when they hand out free ice cream, someone has died and they need the freezer space.

One lunchtime event at sea after Indonesia was a well-attended Aussie barbeque with, naturally, Australian music in the background. There was the obligatory *Waltzing Matilda*, the unofficial national anthem and to many non-Australians an upbeat tune about a jolly man in the bush who does a bit of dancing. In fact, the song is a much darker tale of sheep stealing and death: a swagman camps under a coolibah tree, boils his billy, grabs a jumbuck and shoves it into his tucker bag, but along comes a squatter and three troopers, so the man jumps into a billabong and dies. See what I mean? (Translation, with apologies to our Australian readers: an itinerant worker camps under a eucalyptus tree, boils some water, grabs a passing sheep and shoves it into his food bag, but when a farmer and three policemen challenge him about the sheep, the man jumps into a waterhole and drowns.) The title refers to wandering ('waltzing') with a bundle of belongings (a 'Matilda') on one's back. So, no dancing, and not at all jolly; ultimately creepy, in fact, given that the swagman's ghost is still out there in the bush, inviting you to come a-waltzing.

Other songs booming out at our afternoon barbie, as we speared a few prawns and grabbed a tinny, were raucous Irish-Australian ballads with driving rhythms and anti-colonial themes, so a bit of a shock to our tender English ears. The romance of the rebel sticking it to the English authorities and being free to roam the bush ensured that ballads like *The Wild Colonial Boy* are still popular a hundred and fifty or so years later, even, apparently, with modern-day cruise passengers from middle-class suburbs of Sydney or Melbourne. Our Aussie friends – who sang lustily and seemed to know all the words – laughed it off as just a bit of fun.

The official Australian national anthem is *Advance Australia Fair*, the lyrics of which have changed over time: for some inexplicable reason, lines about the true British courage of the gallant Cook have been erased, as has 'Britannia rules the wave' (fair dinkum, as they say down under, since that's obviously no longer true anyway). However, I was later delighted to find in a Sydney gift shop a bookmark with all the original lyrics, intact.

Meanwhile, the *Amsterdam*'s themed evenings were now coming thick and fast: Oktoberfest, Canadian Thanksgiving, Halloween and Indonesian Night had all been and gone. Guy Fawkes Night, too (aka Bonfire Night). I don't remember what costumes were worn by revellers celebrating the failed plot to blow up the British Parliament 400 years ago, but the crew built realistic-looking bonfires out of wood and paper, with flashing lights inside to simulate flames. The international crowd in the bar may not have understood what that was all about, but they seemed to be enjoying themselves. The global festivities continued one afternoon with famous Australian horse race the Melbourne Cup, broadcast live on screens in the Crow's Nest lounge, which was decked out in pink and green and packed with an excitable crowd dressed to the nines for the occasion.

The Melbourne Cup heralded the next great adventure: Australasia.

PART III: Australasia and home

164

AUSTRALIA

Mrs Verne here. In a way, Australia is more my story, as it was the desire on my part to revisit the now exotic-seeming scenes of my 1950s childhood in Sydney that had sparked the idea of the cruise in the first place. I wanted, if I could, to tread in my immigrant parents' footsteps all those years ago as they disembarked and tried to settle in a strange new world.

Landfall for us well over sixty years later would be Darwin in the Northern Territory (also known as the 'Top End'), followed by a slow sail down the east coast before hitting the great city I could still remember, or at least my bit of it. Here we would finally leave the good old *Amsterdam* and, sorry to say, our new Australian friends, two of whom who were getting off at Brisbane and two carrying on to Melbourne. I was intensely looking forward to seeing Australia, but how did my parents feel when they first arrived in 1954?

Although they were definitely immigrants, they were not actual Ten Pound Poms, the term given to British migrants to Australia after World War II (various unconfirmed explanations existing as to the derivation of 'pom'). The proper Ten Pound Poms were given an assisted passage through a scheme operated by the Australian government – part of its ultimately much regretted 'White Australia' policy – under which adults were charged only ten pounds for the voyage by sea while children travelled free. But, just like the Ten Pound Poms, my parents were certainly migrants in search of a better life: along with so many others in a drab post-war Britain, my father had cast about for employment and thought Australia was the answer. In his case, though, as a newish graduate with a degree in physics, he needed a job to kick-start his career as a scientist.

The possibility of a post came up as a researcher at Sydney's National Standards Laboratory. Australia was a long way away and my mother and father were concerned about leaving their own ageing parents, but this looked like an adventure and they both became wildly excited. There was certainly little to be excited about in dreary old Britain, where rationing was still in force, and the idea of beaches, blue skies and perpetual sunshine was very appealing. At the interview my father was told they really wanted someone more experienced, but was offered the job at a lower salary. He accepted on the spot. Unlike the Ten Pound Poms travelling tourist class (the most basic), he was also lucky enough to be offered first-class passage for the whole family, courtesy of his future employers.

There was only one complication. The sailing date was set for July and a second baby was expected towards the middle of May. That was me, eventually arriving late but safe and sound.

My parents happily prepared for their new life. Letters arrived stamped with 'Australia for your Future', and they truly believed it. Extensive, and expensive, purchases followed for life on board. Travelling first-class meant dressing for dinner, they discovered, and so my mother bought a suitable dress (apparently just the one) and my father invested in his first made-to-measure suit at the then grand cost of £25. His Australian salary had started two weeks before departure, so luckily they were in funds. Travel tickets arrived, including the labels 'Wanted on voyage' and 'Not wanted on voyage', and they got hold of two sea trunks for all their clothing and books and photos and other belongings. For me they bought a canopied pram against the sun, which would go into the hold along with the other luggage not needed during the trip.

On the day of departure our little family of four took the train from Birmingham to London, and from there another train to join the Orient line's *SS Orion* berthed at Tilbury Docks. My parents struggled aboard with suitcases, toddler and new baby – only to discover that my mother and the children were in one cabin whilst my father was in another next door, sharing with a tea planter returning to Bombay. Segregating the sexes on these migrant ships was official policy, for some reason (perhaps in fear of the tropical heat inflaming susceptible passengers). Looking after us for the voyage was cabin steward Ralph, and, following previous advice from experienced travellers, my father immediately tipped him ten pounds. As the ship prepared to depart, the passengers crowded onto the upper decks and threw coloured paper streamers to weeping friends and family on the quayside until, as the ship moved slowly off, the streamers gradually broke and contact with those on shore was at last lost. No-one was there to see my parents off; they had already said farewell to their families in Birmingham. Travelling to Australia in those days must have seemed very final. My father's father, Arthur, who had lost his elder son in the war, thought he would never see his one remaining son again.

The *Orion* was an old ship that had recently been used as a troop carrier. The steel rails on deck were concealed beneath countless layers of white paint and the ornate wooden fittings inside belonged to an earlier age (in fact the Antarctic explorer Apsley Cherry-Garrard, author of *The Worst Journey in the World*, met his future wife while sailing on the *Orion* in the 1930s). Only the dining room was air-conditioned; for air the stuffy cabins had to rely on the louvre vents in the door.

This was a crossing, not a cruise, and shipboard life for my parents was far from idyllic. At six weeks old I was the youngest of about twenty children on board, and occasionally my parents had to call on the help of the ship's doctor and nurse for my various ailments as the ship started to sail through the tropics. My two-year-old big sister had her meals in the special children's dining-room, where the children became increasingly fractious as the temperature climbed. The ship's laundry service was expensive, so my parents did their mountains of washing themselves in the passenger laundries.

They accustomed themselves to the daily routine, beginning at about seven when Ralph appeared with tea and fruit, usually an orange, plus the ship's daily bulletin listing events and entertainments. If arriving at a port, there would be a brochure with history and sightseeing information. The main dining room had two sittings and my parents always took the second breakfast after depositing us in the nursery. A mid-morning snack called elevenses was served on deck, usually beef tea and biscuits or fruit. Lunch was managed in the same way as breakfast and then came dinner, complicated for the adults by the need to dress; this time we children would be left to the mercies of the ship's babysitting service. When at sea the ship's band played in the evenings, and there was dancing or Lotto, a type of bingo. I can't imagine my bookish parents doing either.

The *Orion* called at Gibraltar, Marseilles, Naples, and Port Said before sailing through the Suez Canal to Aden (where my father bought a pair of white sharkskin shoes, then regretted it when he inspected them more closely back on board). After that came Bombay, and Ceylon, as Sri Lanka still was, followed by the nine-day voyage across the Indian Ocean. Landfall was made on the west coast at Fremantle, the port for Perth, before the ship sailed on to Adelaide and Melbourne and finally Sydney. This mammoth voyage with two tiny children in searing heat took nearly five weeks.

In Sydney, a few years after her arrival, my mother wrote an article for an English magazine about her feelings on first setting foot in Australia in 1954:

Six a.m. on board ship, and an air of frantic excitement prevails. As the ship slowly enters Sydney harbour, everyone leaves their last-minute packing and goes up on deck to see the beautiful harbour and the famous Sydney bridge.

The returning Australians tend to become sentimental, and there were many cries of 'Good old Aussie!' from near where we stood.

But what do the 'new Australians', like ourselves, feel? A certain excitement, yes, but also rather a hollow sensation, for most of them know that at the end of this long journey there will be not one soul to recognise and greet them.

It's a most forlorn sensation to stand amongst the baggage by the customs sheds, 12,000 miles from home, trying not to stare at the groups of reunited Australians, kissing and hugging in the good old family way. In fact, despite one's own family to take charge of, it's rather difficult not to think, 'Where's Mother?'

Above all, of course, one wonders, 'What's it going to be like? What problems will we have to face?'

My father, too, wrote about arriving in Australia in a memoir written a few years before he died. There is colour and flavour in his descriptions of the voyage and their new home, and of his feelings leaving his parents and trying to settle in an alien country, but his scientific researches were also much on his mind. Interspersed with the many new impressions there is a great deal of this sort of thing:

... (the paper) undertook to explain the superconductive electronic structure and to predict for metals a second order thermodynamic transition showing the magnetic Meissner effect. Froelich's notion of phonon exchange was assumed to provide an attractive interelectronic attraction and the core of the approach was Cooper's notion of electron 'pairing'.

Not exactly redolent of the sights and sounds of an exotic new continent.

My mother was right to worry that there might be difficulties – plenty, as it turned out. Their first problem was where to live. They stayed for a while at a guest house in Kirribilli, a little suburb within walking distance of the famous Harbour Bridge. A lively mix of other nationalities were staying there too, and my parents began to realise that they were only one of many migrant families seeking a new life in the Australian sunshine. That first weekend, they took my sister and me down to the bridge and wondered what their future would be. Shortly afterwards my father's employer placed us in a flat in the North Shore suburb of Queenscliff, for however long it took us to find a permanent home. It was near Freshwater Beach, where we began to enjoy weekend picnics (not that I remember, still only a few months old and mostly asleep in a pram).

The housing situation for migrants was dire, however. Unless they had at least 1,000 Australian pounds in cash, newcomers could not hope to buy their own home. The Government provided accommodation for migrants up river at Parramatta, and my parents went to have a look. They were horrified – people were living in wooden huts with corrugated iron roofs which must have been unbearably hot in summer. In fact it was Australian policy to make the camps as basic as possible, in order to encourage people to get on their feet and find work and somewhere else to live, although many ended up having to spend long periods there. Some families returned to Britain rather than stay in the camps, with at least a quarter of the British emigrants to Australia after WWII departing for home. A few even refused to get off the ship in the first place. Amongst the Ten Pound Poms, those who chose to return before the mandatory two years had to find not only their fare back, but also to make up the difference between the subsidised £10 passage out and its real cost. Many stayed just long enough to avoid having to do this, becoming what was called 'Boomerang Poms'. Some were so drained financially they had great difficulty rebuilding their lives once back in Britain.

Another option was to rent, but rents were exorbitant. What many did was build their own house, buying a plot of land and building a garage to live in while they erected the house themselves from timberframe kits, at the same time working at their daily job. To my parents this seemed too daunting, and in any case they had no money. They went on looking.

At the Queenscliff flat my mother was thrilled with the ultra-modern fittings and conveniences, so amazing after the shortages of postwar life in Birmingham, but they needed to find their own place. An English work colleague generously offered to lend us enough to make up the collateral sum required by the bank for a loan, and my parents were able to buy their first ever house. A photo from the time shows them posing outside their new bungalow in the suburb of Normanhurst, my father in high-waisted fifties trousers and my mother in a calf-length printed frock, both looking incredibly young.

No. 59 Campbell Avenue, sitting in a dip below the road, had a great gum tree at the front and half an acre of rough land to the rear, big enough for the Dutch immigrants next door to keep horses and chickens. Bordering the land at the very end was what looked like real Australian bush – strictly forbidden to us children. It was a 'fibro' house, made of cement sheets reinforced with asbestos fibres (now banned) and it proved to be just as boiling as the Parramatta huts must have been. No air-conditioning in them days, of course. Our family moved in at exactly the point the really hot weather arrived; the temperature climbed to over 100F and the fibro house heated up like an oven, preventing sleep and causing stomach upsets. The local chemist advised a mixture of kaolin and morphine, and from then on a supply was kept in the house. This was a medicine my mother developed something of a predilection for, swigging it straight from the bottle (the source of years of family jokes about her desperate drug addiction, although researching the mixture now it seems that the morphine in the mixture had no opioid action whatsoever, merely an anti-diarrhoeal effect).

My parents had to buy flyscreens and mosquito netting and began to find the heat increasingly hard to bear. There was a cooling wind sometimes in the early evenings, the 'southerly buster', when the windows would suddenly rattle and let in a delicious breeze. The open windows also allowed Christmas beetles in, large creatures with iridescent bodies that would immediately head towards the bright lights then fall to the floor with burnt wings. After the heat at Christmas came the heavy rains at the end of January, when the house became damp and green mould appeared on books and shoes.

Spiders in the house were common, usually large harmless ones which hid in towels, so that they always had to be examined before use. In the garden and garage, however, were the extremely dangerous funnel-web and redback spiders, and also large ants. One funnel-web in the garage put up a furious fight before my father was finally able to kill it. Ticks – parasitic mites that can cause serious illness and even death in young children – fell on our heads from the trees so that at bath time our hair always had to be checked over. Leeches from the little creek running across the back garden would also latch on to our bare legs, and my father would use a lighted match to make them drop off.

In addition to the heat and the damp there was no sewerage, which at that time, in the mid 1950s, was the case for about half the residential suburbs of Sydney. In some areas the Council permitted septic tanks and luckily our house had one (a photograph of my fourth birthday party rather oddly shows me and a lot of other little girls sitting on it in party hats and sashed 1950s dresses). Unfortunately, our next-door neighbour and several other neighbours did *not* have a septic tank. Each week the 'sani-man' came to bring a new tin and remove the old one. Around his lorry in high summer there was quite an atmosphere, as my mother delicately put it. To my newly arrived, post-war British parents, used to very little in the way of modernity, it seemed strange that so many Australian householders had a car, every conceivable modern device – separate laundry rooms fitted with the latest washing-machines, rotary clothes-drying hoists, refrigerators, floor-polishers, food-mixers, and even the recent luxury of television – but no universal sewerage system. My mother heard about a girl who, when asked what type of engagement ring she wanted, told her fiancé that she would rather he spent his money on a septic tank.

My mother particularly valued our Hills Hoist, the rotary clothes line that you could adjust for height. She had never seen one before coming to Australia; in fact they were invented in Adelaide and became a sort of metaphor for Australian suburbia in the 1950s and 60s. Ours stood next to the septic tank and features in several of our old family photographs, a lone towel hanging limply in the heat or Mother standing proudly beside it. One photograph includes our mangle, a separate device for wringing the water out of the washing, which would be dragged outside from the garage to be nearer the line for hanging. Our luxuries in the house were a bathroom with a good shower – an unfamiliar item to most Britons at the time – a new washing-machine, and a large new fridge. The sitting-room my parents furnished in modern fifties style: coffee tables and armchairs with spindly wooden legs splaying out, rugs on a polished wooden floor, a framed Degas print on the wall.

They settled down, my father taking the 45-minute train journey into Sydney each day – no money for a car, and in any case he couldn't drive – while my mother stayed at home alone looking after a growing brood of very small children. She made friends in the neighbourhood, but was lonely, and increasingly missed her mother and friends back in Birmingham. In fact they were both homesick: on occasional visits to Circular Quay in the city, both would gaze longingly at the home-bound ships. But there was no way to return, so they tried to make the best of things. She still collected magazine items about the difficulties experienced by immigrants, and in her own articles expressed regret for never having fully appreciated the English press and the BBC. She wrote home often, and would cut out the pictures of snowy winter scenes from newspapers sent over by her family. She worked to prevent us acquiring a strong Australian accent, refusing to let us listen to a particular children's presenter on the radio who had very strident tones. All of this, of course, speaks to an unwillingness to see Australia as her home – although, just before our family's one trip back to England in the middle of the seven years in Sydney, she did write wistfully of the brightness of the local golden wattle trees just coming into bloom, and how she would miss the jacarandas.

Now, returning to my childhood home at last, I planned to take that same suburban train out to Normanhurst to find the old fibro house and try to imagine the life my mother and father had led there but ultimately put behind them. In 1959 my father was offered a senior lectureship at the University of New South Wales but, as he wrote later, 'to accept this meant committing ourselves to Australia and this we were still not ready for'. Despite these words, he believed that after our return from that single visit to England my mother had begun to view life in Australia more favourably. In a year or two, he wrote in his memoir, they would accept the life once and for all. There was even half a plan to move from Normanhurst to the better climate in Katoomba in the Blue Mountains, from where daily commuting would be possible.

But by January 1960, when there was a particularly brutal heatwave, the heat was really getting to my mother. It felt like a hot fog, like being trapped in a cupboard of hot blankets, she wrote. Gastroenteritis ripped through the family again and we were unable to enjoy iced lemonade from our exciting new blender because lemons made our stomachs worse. Despite the heatwave, she was shocked by free-and-easy Australian friends who, when visiting our house, would walk over to the fridge and help themselves to a drink without asking.

The following year my father decided to accept an offer of a year's work in America, all of us first sailing to England on the *SS Orontes* for a quick visit to family. We packed up and, in October 1961, boarded ship at Circular Quay.

The house in Normanhurst was let out for our year of absence, but we never returned.

Darwin

Australia is a place where you can enjoy the finest cuisine, exquisite wines, world-class opera and ballet, fine art galleries and museums – and then, merely by straying off a pathway, get devoured by a crocodile, python, dingo or great white shark.

(Kathy Lette, Sydney-born writer)

Sixty years or so later, and we were reaching Darwin. Incredibly hot and, although I had never been to Darwin as a child, just the sensation and scent of the air and the sound of the birds immediately felt like coming home. Australia *was* home, up to the age of seven. After our long tour of Asia, there was the added familiarity of people speaking English and leading lives similar to our own, even in that exotic air. In the wake of some of the difficulties we had encountered in other cultures through the very differentness of it all, it was a relief simply to find an appropriate shop, choose a koala-plastered birthday card for our son back home, buy a stamp at a post office and post it, all within the space of half an hour with no problems whatsoever. We celebrated with coffee and cake at an outside café – a mistake, it turned out, in 91-degree heat, and definitely a mistake when we got the bill. Australia at that time was extremely expensive.

Darwin had been badly bombed in the war. Over a period of several months in 1942 and 1943 the Japanese attack force that had devastated Pearl Harbor also bombed Australia's northernmost city; at least three hundred people were killed on the first day. In 1974 poor Darwin was also 70% destroyed by Cyclone Tracy, but after all the trauma it was now a thriving modern metropolis with plenty of banyan and other trees providing welcome shade. The beaches are closed between October and May – jellyfish – but some very red locals were floating in pools by the waterfront, slowly baking under the broiling sun (in fact 'sun baking' is the Australian term for sunbathing). This did not seem like the best idea and we opted instead for Darwin's excellent (and free) Museum and Art Gallery, where we enjoyed a whole room dedicated to all the things that can kill you in Australia. I remembered my mother talking about her horror when given a list of the deadly spiders and insects she needed to watch out for, something all those breezy brochures from Australia House had omitted to mention amidst the lyrical descriptions of golden beaches and sunny skies. She had had literally no idea you could die from a spider bite, and would probably never have set foot in Australia if she had.

As we wandered around the town, admiring the lovely white blossom of the frangipani trees, we started to notice the indigenous people of Darwin politely acceding to requests for photographs from some of our strolling fellow tourists. The locals were presumably members of the Larrakia Aboriginal tribe, said to 'own' the area. One of our Australian friends on the boat, a social worker accustomed to working with indigenous communities, had mentioned government handouts spent on drink and people passing out in the streets, but here there seemed only folk going quietly about their business and groups of smiling, neatly dressed schoolgirls. Three older women were happy to tell us the way to the famous banyan known as the 'Tree of Knowledge', an historic meeting place and trading spot (which admittedly did have some empty bottles underneath, but that could have been anybody). I have no memory of ever seeing an aboriginal person during my Australian childhood, although looking it up now I find that the percentage of the population in Sydney is low. There were certainly no indigenous girls at my primary school.

Time was now ebbing away for us in Darwin and it became obvious we wouldn't make it to Crocosaurus Cove aquarium as planned – desperate as we were to engage with some crocodiles after finding several shocking stories in a local newspaper about croc attacks, penned by their dedicated crocodile and UFO reporter. 'Croc Found in Kids' Sandpit', 'What a Croc!' and 'Fisho Inches from Death' – that sort of thing. The Northern Territory even has a Be Crocwise initiative advising how to reduce the risk of croc attacks while camping, fishing or swimming (as if). In the UK we're used to public safety campaigns on a much smaller scale, like 'Find a tick? Remove it quick'. I had to drag Mr Verne away from the historic site of the First Overland Telegraph Pole, complete with its photo of the 'planting' ceremony in 1870 and background information ('When finished, the line stretched for 2,000 miles north to south ... ', at which point I stopped reading). After searching a super-cool air-conditioned supermarket for a kettle, it was back to the *Amsterdam* for another in a long line of cooling showers capping off a day of hot and dusty discovery. I was already delighted with Australia, so far a lovely mix (for us) of old-fashioned Britishness in a heady atmosphere of informality, hot sunshine, and the screeching of colourful birds, everything tinged by awakened memories. Trying to explain my feelings to our Aussie friends at dinner that evening, I was overcome with emotion.

A day at sea after Darwin, and a chance to catch up on laundry (me) and to rest (guess who – his excuse being that his back was still stiff and he needed to relax before his big day at the Great Barrier Reef). Laundry was a do-it-yourself affair as we hadn't yet qualified for the ship's free service. We already had 3-star 'Mariner' status, having completed more than 75 cruise days with HAL before embarking the *Amsterdam*, but unfortunately this doesn't grant you many perks: 25% off wine packages, 10% off HAL-logo clothing, and (gosh) a complimentary photo of the ship. We were a long way off earning 4-star status (= 200 cruise days), which gives you 50% off wine packages, the coveted free laundry service, and priority boarding and tendering. When HAL celebrated its 150th anniversary in 2023, a few dozen top Mariners – guests with an unimaginable 1,400 or more cruise days – got to rub shoulders with Princess Margriet of the Netherlands. No disrespect, but give me the free laundry any day.

For many of its cruise segments Holland America invites Cultural Ambassadors to come on board and talk about the local region, perform, teach crafts, and so on. Disappointingly for us (and no doubt to the relief of Aussie passengers), for Australia this was not Sir Les Patterson, the boorish, drunken cultural attaché character so often a part of Australian comedian Barry Humphries' stage act. Instead, some Aboriginal traditional dancers gave us a fantastic performance.

Entries in the photo competition had now been on display and the votes were in. Mr Verne's kimono ladies on a train platform did attract votes, but not enough to win a prize. I suspect foul play.

Great Barrier Reef and Brisbane

...off the port bow I can see a good 150 solid citizens floating face-down, motionless, looking like the massed and bloated victims of some hideous mishap – from this height it's a macabre and riveting sight.

(David Foster Wallace, *Harpers* magazine)

On we sailed down the east coast, all too conscious now that our magical trip on the *Amsterdam* was nearly at an end. To make up for the disappointment over Papua New Guinea the shipping line had decided to put into Hamilton Island, a beautiful spot off the Queensland coast that serves as a jumping off point – not literally – for snorkelling and scuba diving on the Great Barrier Reef. Basically a water sports resort for extremely rich people, Hamilton allows no cars, only golf carts (and plenty of very expensive shops). I explored the tiny island with a 10-minute bus tour right round it, then paddled happily on the paradisiacal Catseye Beach before coming across a rather hidden away notice about jellyfish stings: '...if you experience muscle pain and difficulty breathing, seek immediate medical help'. Mr Verne, meanwhile, had catamaranned out to the Reef at vast expense to don wetsuit, snorkel, flippers and flotation jacket, look very silly, then along with dozens of his fellow passengers float gently around the coral walls being an object of curiosity for darting shoals of brightly coloured fish. No sharks, thankfully, despite all those scary stories about the Australian coast. He saw fish nibbling on the coral, clams gently opening and closing, and a large maori wrasse that liked to be stroked, gliding hopefully by.

The good ship *Amsterdam* ploughed on through the turquoise waters between coast and reef to Brisbane, our last stop before disembarkation. Seven weeks aboard now and no murders (that we knew of). The day at sea between two stops finished with another themed evening at dinner, this time Casino night, a golden opportunity for more outrageous dressing up. Simple-minded, but great fun.

Brisbane

Brisbane, once we had sailed up the river of the same name and the ship had parked only four miles from the city centre, was to be the setting for our first encounter with kangaroos, koalas, emus, wombats and cassowaries. At the Lone Pine Koala Sanctuary not far from the city we found both the kangaroos and koalas startlingly tame, with the koalas (smelling strongly of their diet of eucalyptus leaves) quite happy to be cuddled for photographs. This is a privilege allowed only in Queensland, and carefully controlled. Each koala is only available for 30 minutes per day, two days on, one day off.

The kangaroos, too, were willing to be petted and have people approach their young up close. We were surprised to see that at least on this occasion the baby kangaroos, or joeys, were not sitting in the mother's pouch with head poking cutely out as forever depicted, but had dived into the pouch head first so that all you saw was a pair of feet and a tail hanging out.

When it rained, we tourists sought cover in a little corrugated iron shelter and so did several kangaroos, who came pounding up wanting to get out of the wet just as much as we did. They waited patiently outside till the penny dropped and we shuffled aside to make space for them, at which point they hopped politely in and began snacking from a trough. It was all very civilised.

> • **Mr Verne's fun facts:** The female kangaroo's pouch may hold young at different stages of their development, so she has four teats and can produce a different type of milk for each. The name koala is Aboriginal for 'no water', since a koala gets moisture from chewing eucalyptus leaves. While it's still young a koala joey feeds on its mother's 'pap', a type of faeces that contains bacteria useful for digesting the leaves.

Brisbane itself was an attractive, stylish, modern city still retaining some older Victorian buildings of reddish stone with ornate ironwork balconies. The jacaranda trees were wonderfully pretty, their mauve blossoms looking like upside down bluebells.

In our first lesson in Australian at a coffee shop we learned that our usual Americano order translated to 'strong long black', and, as we also later learned, their Tim Tam snacks were none other than Britain's beloved Penguin biscuits.

One final day at sea, spent washing, packing, and saying our farewells not only to new friends, but also to all the personnel who had looked after us so well in cabin and dining room for a voyage of fifty nights. Other passengers, too, were hugging their stewards and waiters and taking photographs. On a long journey in such close quarters it's certainly possible to form warm relationships – but would passengers and ship's crew alike really remember each other after a few months had passed? Hard to say.

The moment had arrived. We had totally loved the *Amsterdam* – just the right size not to be overwhelmed by too many fellow passengers, good food with interesting Indonesian touches, good lectures – and, best of all, no exclamation marks in the information bulletins. We were very sorry to leave her behind, if delighted to reach Sydney at last, and the *Amsterdam* lingers in our memory as the best ship we ever sailed on. Covid-19 later caused her 2020 World Cruise to be abandoned mid-way, with all passengers having to somehow make their way home from Australia in stressful circumstances. It was soon after announced that the ship had been sold to Fred Olsen, who renamed it *Bolette* and did a refit, promising that the ship would have a 'quintessentially English feel'. We didn't like the sound of that. What did it mean? Orderly queues, warm beer, bad food, endless *Downton Abbey* on TV and live cricket shown in the sports bar? Whatever it meant, we were betting that the ship would not be as stylish as during its Holland America heyday.

Sydney (and beyond)

...outside my window a misty afternoon drizzle gently but inexorably soaks the City of London. In Sydney Harbour, twelve thousand miles away and ten hours from now, the yachts will be racing on the crushed diamond water under a sky the texture of powdered sapphires...

(Clive James, *Unreliable Memoirs*)

No one in Sydney ever wastes time debating the meaning of life – it's getting yourself a water frontage. People devote a lifetime to the quest.

(David Williamson, *Emerald City*)

My arrival in Sydney, over sixty years after my parents, was of course quite different. No demanding young children, no longing for home and family left far behind, possibly forever. This time I was able to appreciate the spectacular setting of the world's largest natural harbour as the *Amsterdam* cruised slowly through. On the hilly northern shoreline were fabulous houses with sun-drenched balconies, while to the south the business district thrust skywards. Our resident travel expert provided a running commentary, and Opera Rolls and orange juice were served (a HAL in-joke, the rolls being the same anywhere in the world, as we had found with the Panama Rolls and Elephant Island Buns of previous trips). Then, suddenly, as we rounded a headland the Harbour Bridge and Opera House came into full view. I might have become emotional again but do you know, I was below decks doing last-minute packing while certain other people were taking photographs.

After strong warnings from the ship, we decided we would come clean to Australian customs about our wood carvings and the half-eaten bar of chocolate we were bringing in, but in the event we were waved through with easy informality, despite the very visible 'We find, you're fined' posters. Of course most of the earliest British arrivals in Australia were convicts, sent to Australia in the eighteenth and nineteenth centuries for terrible crimes like stealing a handkerchief. Customs did ask if we had criminal records, to which we replied that we hadn't realised you still needed one (this is officially the oldest joke in the world, and by law it has to be included in any account of entering Australia).

It was still early in the morning. The studio with kitchen and washer/dryer we had booked on the 27th floor of a modern high-rise 'boutique' hotel on the edge of Sydney's China Town – which made Sydney initially seem like a continuation of our trip around southeast Asia – was not yet ready, so we left our luggage mountain with them and headed to the Tourist Information Centre. Our initial reconnoitre at the hotel had revealed that the big bucks we were paying did not include wifi, and we wondered if we could find a better deal somewhere. But no. Big bucks and paying yet more

188

on top for wifi was standard. After a period at the fancy high-rise we moved to a more modest hotel in Woolloomooloo, an area near notorious Kings Cross with its 'lively' nightlife (as euphemistically described in most tourist guides, although one did bluntly declare that Sydney's red-light district was frequented by sailors from the Woolloomooloo naval base, and its streets prowled by prostitutes, drug abusers, drunks and homeless teenagers). In the new hotel the staff were green young students who had seemingly never made a bed, which we discovered on the first night when all the bedclothes erupted onto the floor with the slightest movement. Around the hotel we were to see people sleeping rough in the streets, some of them bedding down for the night beneath an underpass.

> • **Mr Verne's fun facts:** Woolloomooloo was formerly a working-class area with a rowdy reputation, hence expressions like 'Woolloomooloo upper-cut' (a kick in the groin), a distant cousin of the Scottish 'Glasgow kiss' (headbutt). No doubt unaware of its notoriety Mark Twain described Woolloomooloo as 'the most musical and gurgly' of names, being particularly impressed, as we all should be, that it contains eight Os.

That first day was spent wandering around Circular Quay, the harbour's cruise and ferry terminal framed by the iconic, white-sailed Opera House on one side and the equally famous bridge on the other. The

Quay is prime tourist country, studded with photo opportunities such as the Aboriginal tribal member in full rig and paint playing the didgeridoo wind instrument, and Writers Walk, a series of circular metal plaques embedded in the ground celebrating famous Australian writers. These included our new all-time favourite poem, Barry Humphries' ode to a meat pie, which begins:

I think that I could never spy

A poem lovely as a pie.

A banquet in a single course

Blushing with rich tomato sauce.

(From *Piece in the Form of a Meat Pie*)

Brings a tear to the eye. But dammit, those Aussie meat pies are good. After eating one later on our way to the Snowy Mountains, Mr Verne said it was the best meat pie he had ever had in his life. I think he *was* crying.

Not far from Circular Quay is the Rocks, an arty sort of area in the shadow of the bridge composed of boutiques, traditional houses and a local history museum inside a tiny old cottage. The rows of historic houses were delightful: pretty wrought iron balconies and railings, stuccoed fronts, and rounded tops to the doors and windows. As we climbed a steep hill lined with these characteristic old Sydney homes we were continually passed by fitness fanatics bounding up and down the steps in the considerable heat, while at the summit there appeared to be a kind of boot camp in progress. No thanks. From there we could see a line of tiny figures moving slowly up the actual arch of the Harbour Bridge. If you're mad enough, the cost of a 3-hour bridge climb tour is about $US 220, including official photos (no cameras or phones allowed; they don't want some butter-fingers dropping them on passing cars and pedestrians). We descended to the Rocks Market area for a simple al fresco lunch, while taking in the lively scene around us. (This included a colourful clothes stall opposite the café run by a tall, elegant Asian lady with a very prominent Adam's apple, and why not.) Later, we enjoyed the first decent cup of tea we had had in two months: the milk used on the ship had given it a funny taste.

The centre of Sydney was similar to any large city – skyscrapers, a business district – and it's the huge, sparkling, ferry-crossed harbour and leafy suburbs that provide its character. In many places in both suburbs and city we found more of those old Victorian terraced houses with the iron lacework balconies, often shaded by the wonderful jacaranda trees gently shedding their mauve blossoms to carpet the pavement below. The scent of honeysuckle and the screech of exotic birds make it half city, half tropical paradise, and all the more dream-like for the many familiar London place names bestowed so long ago by English settlers: Kings Cross, Paddington, Oxford St, Bayswater Rd, Lewisham, Bondi Beach ... OK, maybe not Bondi Beach. That's *very* Australian.

In 1960, when I was six, my father took a family picture on the harbour bridge. By then I had a little sister and a brother, the first boy in the family, enthusiastically welcomed by my father after all those girls. (His exact words in his memoir were as follows: 'While I would have been happy to have had a fourth daughter I was proud and delighted to have achieved a son, and enjoyed the congratulations that eventually followed.' Thanks, Dad.) Anyway, in the picture on the bridge our mother stands at the back and we three sisters are in front in our matching pinafore dresses, me holding my skirt out in a kind of curtsy pose, with my brother in his pushchair. In black and white, it's an evocative photo, at least for me, although the composition could be better: there is absolutely nothing visible of the beautiful harbour itself, merely some prongs of ironwork sticking out that might just identify it as the famous bridge.

Before embarking on our odyssey we had decided to recreate this photograph and several others taken all those years previously by my father, a keen amateur photographer who developed his own 'snaps', as they were then called, in our blacked-out kitchen at night. The photo on the bridge may not have been ideally arranged but many others were wonderful, especially one of my older sister and me holding hands on a breezy hilltop in the Blue Mountains. The mad plan now was for Mr Verne, also an excellent photographer, to take shots of me five decades later in the same locations and, if possible, in the same pose. Off we set along the bridge, looking for the precise location of the original photograph. Perhaps somewhat arbitrarily – bits of ironmongery all looking much the same without any other reference points – we stopped at what seemed the right spot and I turned to face the camera. As you might imagine if you gave it more thought than we did, taking a finicky shot amidst a constant stream of Japanese tourists proved to be a tad tricky, never mind how silly a woman of mature years looks holding out her skirt like Little Bo Peep. Every time I assumed the position, another gaggle of teenaged girls in Hello Kitty backpacks would surge up behind me and ruin the shot. We finally managed it, and the resultant recreation of a lost moment became the first of a gallery of such re-enactments for me to share with the siblings who had featured in the original. They included a shot in delightfully leafy Kirribilli on the far side of the bridge, where my parents had briefly stayed on their arrival, and another on Freshwater Beach, though this was pretty hard to recreate because in the 1950s photo I had been nothing more than a mound of blankets being fed a bottle by my mother sitting in the sand.

Katoomba was later to be the scene of another such re-enactment. I vividly remembered our holidays there, although not the very first time my family visited this scenic mountain town about a hundred miles inland of Sydney, where it was cooler. Their first Australian Christmas had been spent – or nearly spent – in a hotel there called the Sans Souci. My parents were just admiring the beautiful blue haze in the valley out of their bedroom window when they suddenly realised that the stunning colour was actually due to burning trees: a serious bushfire was ripping towards them. By the next morning all available manpower had been summoned to help contain it, each man wielding a long brush of twigs to use as a broom to beat down the leaping flames – just one flying spark would ignite the dry and oily gum trees into scary, blazing columns. The hotel closed down and our holiday was over, but there was more drama to come. As they resignedly packed up for the return to Sydney, my parents noticed suspicious spots on my sister's face and arms. Chicken pox. The holiday would have been curtailed in any case. They wrapped her in shawls, bundled me into the pram, and hurried to the station to catch the train, thankful to be heading out of the danger zone. Then, after only a few minutes, the train ground to a halt: the wooden rail-sleepers ahead were on fire and the train had to be evacuated. As they handed us children down onto the track they could see the burning sleepers ahead. My sister's spots were now the least of their troubles, but somehow they got us, themselves and their belongings onto a relief bus to a more secure part of the line where another train was waiting, and finally left the danger behind. By this point, no doubt, longing for Birmingham.

Subsequent holidays in Katoomba – yes, incredibly, they went back – were less traumatic, and I can remember the hotel, and seeing the Three Sisters rocks at Echo Point, and my father pushing us on the swings in a park. (He used to go off into a corner at the hotel to read a book, and one of the other guests remarked to my mother that her husband seemed rather odd.) Now, on our photographic odyssey some sixty years later, we found that the Sans Souci hotel had become a nursing home but the Three Sisters were of course still there, just about visible through the fog of a rainy day. We had been told as children of the ancient Aboriginal legend that they were the daughters of a chieftain turned to stone, but now as an adult I discovered, disappointingly, that this was a story fabricated to encourage tourism.

We also found the swings near Leura Kiosk where I had swung as a child, and looked for the exact spot where my father had taken my favourite photograph in the whole world, my big sister and I holding hands, our hair streaming in the wind, a gum tree swaying behind us.

The day came for the return to the old house in Normanhurst, last seen at the age of seven on the day we left Australia for ever. I remembered the house very well. A wooden ramp led up the side of it, levelling off at the top where the kitchen door and the front door rather strangely stood next to each other. Here on the flat part of the ramp my mother would carry out some task like shelling peas, sitting in the kitchen doorway in the sunshine next to the huge pram from England airing the latest baby. In very hot weather the ramp was cooler at night than inside the house, and my father would sometimes sleep out there.

We took a commuter train, travelling through Sydney's northern suburbs just as my father had done every day to his workplace in the beautiful grounds of Sydney University. The names of some of these Northern Line stations rang bells – Beecroft, Pennant Hills. We got out at Normanhurst Station, which I could also remember – waiting there with my mother for the steam train, frightening enough to a young child with its belching smoke and whistling to make me dive under the bench whenever it approached. As we stepped out onto the platform I suddenly recognised the laughing call of kookaburras, a sound that instantly transported me back across the years. Then on to Campbell Avenue along the busy main road, now a thunderous six-lane highway, the road along which my sister and I had walked on our own to school. Surely not the same road? But it was.

The twists and turns as we walked down Campbell Avenue, fortunately still quiet and leafy, seemed just as long as when I was a little girl walking home at the end of the day. I looked for the little bridge over the stream just before number 59, but there was no sign of it. Not only that, but with a sense of shock, I saw that the old fibro house itself had gone, and in its place were modern flats. Even the spreading gum tree at the top of our old drive seemed to have vanished, scene of a memorable incident with a disturbed nest of soldier ants that ran all over my bare feet in their open-toe sandals. The wild bush at the back of our long garden, so strictly forbidden to us children, had been built over.

Things change, I know. It was amazing enough that even after sixty years Campbell Avenue was still much as it used to be. But it felt as though my parents, bewildered and homesick in a strange new country, had simply been wiped from the earth along with the house.

After a while we'd done a great deal in and around Sydney, including the fantastic Opera House (well all right, a brief sortie into the gift shop). Now we wanted to explore even further: it was time to go walkabout.

First we needed to jettison some of our mountain of luggage and, just for once, try to travel light. We tracked down somewhere to store the bulk of our stuff for a week or so and chatted to the man behind the counter at the little check-in office.

'So, what happens to it from here?' I asked idly, thinking the suitcases would likely be taken on to some larger facility.

'I take it out the back and go through it looking for anything valuable,' he replied without missing a beat.

Australia! I loved it!

And now I will hand back to Mr Verne, as he's been straining to be let off the leash.

Mr Verne Hits the Outback

We're all members of the outback club, We don't back down and we don't give up. We're all living in the land we love...

(Lee Kernaghan, Australian country music singer – chorus from *The Outback Club*)

Australia lives with a strange contradiction – our national image of ourselves is one of the Outback, and yet nearly all of us live in big cities. Move outside the coastal fringe, and Australia can feel like a foreign country.

(Kate Grenville, author)

OK, I hit the outback *with* Mrs Verne. No choice.

In Sydney we had bought unlimited travel passes to go further afield – to Manly Beach across the harbour by ferry, Bondi Beach by train and bus, and Parramatta along the mangrove-lined river west of the harbour. As a World Surfing Reserve, Manly boasted '100 years of surfing heritage', one surprising early fan being Sherlock Holmes author Sir Arthur Conan Doyle in 1920: 'We all devoted ourselves to surf-bathing, spending a good deal of our day in the water as is the custom of the place. It is a real romp with Nature.' Soft golden sand curved around the bay, athletic young people cavorted at volleyball nets, and surf boards were stacked down by the water. A group of wetsuited figures carried boards out into the surf past the 'Danger – strong current' sign. Mrs V had a brief paddle in the cool shallows.

Bondi Beach was unexpectedly low-key: not babes and bodybuilders, but ordinary people enjoying themselves on the beach and in the surf, and Bondi's iconic lifeguards standing ready in their bright yellow and red uniforms (and broad-brimmed hats against the sun). Bondi gets livelier on Australia Day in late January, with fireworks, bonfires, barbeques and booze as the summer holiday season draws to a close.

But there was more to discover.

Days 1-3 (late November)

Once free of at least some of the luggage we took an overnight train west from Sydney to the old mining town of Broken Hill, 700 miles away and still in New South Wales, but suddenly much hotter. Peeping through the train blinds in the dawn hours we had had our first glimpse of what looked like outback: a flat open expanse without habitation, just the odd fence, a few sheep and sheep station signs, the occasional red dirt track seemingly leading to nowhere, and a single kangaroo standing staring at the train. Also the bizarre sight of a family of emus walking in line across the desert. (We arrived at our destination four hours late, following a late departure from Sydney. Still, after Amtrak, we could do four hours standing on our heads.) In Broken Hill itself the streets were all creatively named after minerals: Bromide St, Sulphide St, and so on.

 Our motel was on romantic Chloride St – a popular choice with honeymooners, no doubt. There was not too much to do in Broken Hill, where the clocks had stopped in 1952 and most of the shops were shut most of the time – a feature common to many outback towns, we were to discover – although I got rather overexcited when let loose in a shop selling stones and bits of old rock. Australia's 'Silver City' contains one of the world's largest deposits of silver, lead and zinc and has made a few owners and shareholders fabulously wealthy ever since the late 1800s, but the strikingly modern and very moving Miner's Memorial was a reminder of the risks for the working man: perched on a huge slag heap towering over the town, the memorial listed the name, age and cause of death – 'hit by drill steel', 'buried by mullock', 'crushed by rail truck' – of all 800 or so men (and some boys) who lost their lives in the mines over the years.

Days 4-6

After a day or two we rented a car to drive even further into the bush, to the Flinders Ranges National Park in South Australia, recommended to us by an

Aussie lady encountered in the laundry on the *Amsterdam*. Driving along the very samey, empty road we passed so many kangaroos, emus, and wild goats that after a while we scarcely bothered turning round.

Cars were much rarer – only about one an hour, on average. With no other traffic on the road we gradually began accelerating without realising it, and then got stopped by a police car for speeding (120 in a 110 km/h zone). Playing the innocent I managed to wangle my way out of it and was let off with a caution; otherwise, it would have been a fine of several hundred dollars. At a roadhouse later on I was told I'd been luckier than outlaw Ned Kelly – imposing fines was apparently a prime source of income for the local authorities. Of course Ned Kelly was eventually caught and hanged, so after that we drove quite slowly.

Passing Winnininnie, Oodla Wirra and Orroroo we arrived at our campsite, 250 miles down the road at Hawker. This proved to be pretty basic – the TV in our boiling hot cabin only had three channels (we were furious). When we asked why the caravan park was almost empty, the owner said it was now too hot for people to come here on holiday. Next day it was sunny and 107 degrees (42C), so like true Englishmen we went out in the midday sun for a nice walk to see Yourambulla Caves, famed for their Aboriginal art.

On arriving at the caves after a drive and a steepish climb I was happy to do some climbing up ladders to get to the paintings, but Mrs Verne made the fatal error of going on ahead, and instantly lost the track. Her own private walkabout hell ended about ten minutes later when she picked up the trail again, but still, for a while there it was touch and go – including a tense moment when a sound of heavy crashing about behind her turned out to be a rather large kangaroo. I never did catch her up and when she found herself first back down at the car, luckily with the keys, she hung a shirt out of the window as a signal in case I could see it from afar and would know to stop searching for her. ('*If* you were,' she added darkly.)

Of course, what Mrs V should have done before wandering off into the bush was to *be prepared*. A few simple steps, that's all, like wear sturdy boots and a hat, apply sunscreen, carry two litres of water and enough food for two days, and pack a first aid kit, matches, a detailed map, compass, whistle and HF radio compatible with the Royal Flying Doctor Service. Well, she did put on some sunscreen and a hat. Going missing in the outback is a whole sub-genre in Australian cinema: most famously, *Walkabout* (two children get lost), *Picnic at Hanging Rock* (four girls wander off); and *Jindabyne* (no spoilers – you'll have to watch it). We've written a screenplay about Mrs V's brush with death and submitted it to Australian cinema.

Days 7-8

We drove back to Broken Hill, completing our 600-mile outback tour, then returned to Sydney by overnight train to rent yet another car for the next segment of seeing Australia: a circular route down the coast from Sydney, inland to the Snowy Mountains, up to the capital Canberra and back to Sydney via the Blue Mountains – around 900 miles in all, and yet just a tiny corner of the continent.

Down the Coast

Days 9-13

To Botany Bay, about twenty miles south of Sydney. In a little national park there, a plaque marks where Captain Cook first made landfall in 1770, and there's a monument to botanist Joseph Banks, whose work in collecting so many new plants led to the choice of name for the bay. We were reminded that this was Aboriginal land, though the 'soundscape' of adults talking to their children about their heritage, broadcast from speakers in the foliage, seemed intrusive in this otherwise beautiful, peaceful location. Trails led down to the curving shoreline, pine trees gave shade, birds sang, kookaburras laughed, and there were few visitors. Cook had liked it too – his favourable description of the area, and of the natives' timidity, later influenced the British government to choose Botany Bay for their new penal colony (America, having revolted, was no longer an option and neither was New Zealand, where the Maori were too fierce). And yet, despite what everybody has ever told you, Botany Bay was never used to host convicts. When the First Fleet with its cargo of transportees arrived in 1788, the site was immediately rejected in favour of a much better one a short way up the coast – Sydney Cove, now Circular Quay, where cruise ships tie up and ferries set out across the harbour.

There is a Fellowship of First Fleeters for descendants of those who came over in 1788, which suggests that an old stigma has largely gone away ('None wanted to have convict ancestors, and few could be perfectly sure that some felon did not perch like a crow in their family tree,' wrote Robert Hughes in *The Fatal Shore,* his history of the origins of Australia), though if your ancestor was transported for murder rather than petty theft, you might want to keep it to yourself.

Further down the coast, the area around Jervis Bay was pure English countryside but with a twist: emu oil or peaches were being sold by the roadside, and at a rest stop 'dunny' – toilet – a sign instructed you to lower the seat lid because worms were employed to break down waste matter, and 'worms work better in the dark'. In town, a pharmacy offered Kangaroo Essence for Men (enhances men's 'stamina') and Sheep Placenta (rejuvenates your skin). A rooftop Santa's sleigh was being pulled by six kangaroos, and a wooden Santa outside a store held a surf board showing the number of days until Christmas.

Day 14

Eden, in the south-east corner of New South Wales, had been a whaling station for a hundred years until 1930. The local museum told a remarkable story: for decades, a pod of orcas would herd humpback whales together in the bay and block their escape, then thrash the water as a signal to the men on shore, who would launch their rowboats, harpoon in hand *Moby-Dick* style. As a reward, the orcas were allowed to feast on the slaughtered humpbacks' tongues and lips, the only part they wanted. The skeleton of the last of these killer whales – Old Tom – was on display in the museum, while the whalers' descendants were now running whale-watching trips. (Back up the coast a lady in the tourist office had told us that we were just too late in the season to see whales migrating south, and what a fantastic season it had been. Tact obviously not her strength.)

Another remarkable tale from Eden was that in the late 1800s, whale carcasses provided a novel treatment for rheumatism. Large holes would be cut in a whale's flanks for sufferers to sit in for up to 30 hours with just their heads poking out, the theory being that warmly decomposing blubber relieved rheumatic pains. One definite after-effect was that these poor people gave off a 'horrible dead odour' for weeks afterwards.

Round the bay was the site of the old whaling station. Little remains to be seen on the deserted shore, but at one time there would have been tables for cutting up the blubber, and furnaces and vats for boiling and distilling the whale oil – arduous, smelly, greasy work, now a thankfully distant memory.

The Interior

Days 15-16

Jindabyne, the Snowy Mountains, early December. Our hotel was virtually empty, at which point we realised that in the eyes of the natives we had been late for the outback (too hot), early for the coast (summer holidays start after Christmas), and off season for the Snowy Mountains, where ski resorts were currently closed. Not that we had any desire to go skiing. Instead, we drove up to a high point and hiked a winding trail down to the Snowy River, passing white-barked snowgums and alpine wildflowers peeping out from patches of snow across the boggy hillside.

Day 17

North to Canberra, and a visit to Parliament House, on Capital Hill. Actually, it's built *into* the hill, its roof covered with grass and sprouting an enormously high steel flagpole as if to remind citizens where their parliament is. Above the entrance was Australia's coat of arms, a kangaroo and emu facing each other on either side of a shield. In the impressive foyer, green and pink marble pillars represented a forest of eucalyptus trees, floors were made from native woods, and marquetry on wall panels depicted native flora. While Australia may be a modern, progressive society, its Parliament has many traditions that are based on the British model, including even an Usher of the Black Rod, who used to wear buckled shoes, britches and a lace ruff, but now just a boring old suit. The names of the Parliament's two houses would be familiar to any visitor from the USA: House of Representatives and Senate.

By contrast, in front of the Old Parliament House nearby was the Aboriginal Tent Embassy. A small hut now rather than tent, it first appeared in 1972 as a protest against the lack of land rights for Aboriginal peoples, and has survived the fifty-plus years since, despite arson attacks and political opposition. Remarkably, in 2004 the Embassy was officially registered as an important place of national heritage.

Other reconciliation efforts include the annual Sorry Day, which acknowledges the generations of Aboriginal children forcibly removed from their families 'for their own good' (*Hands up if you're sorry*, read one poster in Sydney), and the practice of reading out a respectful Acknowledgement of Country statement at the start of any kind of gathering, from nursery children to boardrooms to weddings. Websites, TV programmes and movies also begin with an Acknowledgement statement.

The wording varies according to location, and in the case of the bridge climb tour operator back in Sydney this had read:

BridgeClimb acknowledges the Gadigal people of the Eora Nation, the Traditional Owners of the land on which BridgeClimb operates. We pay our respects to all First Nations people and acknowledge Elders past and present.

(The label 'Aborigine' is increasingly deemed offensive, the preferred term being 'Aboriginal peoples' because the many different Aboriginal groups should not be lumped together as one.)

Day 18

Breaking out into the countryside again, we zigzagged north. I casually mentioned to Mrs V that I was taking a slight detour to a place called Cootamundra but didn't say why, for fear of my plan being vetoed; all was revealed by the huge sign outside town announcing it as the birthplace of Donald Bradman, the famous cricketer. I headed straight for the cottage-sized museum dedicated to his memory. Not a cricket fan, Mrs V waited reasonably patiently outside in the car. When Bradman died in 2001 at the age of 92, *The Sydney Morning Herald*'s headline was 'The Don – a nation mourns', above a cartoon of God asking for his autograph as he passes through the Pearly Gates. Given the ancient, intense rivalry between the Australia and England cricket teams (one Aussie fast bowler in the 1970s used to relish hitting batsmen with the ball: 'I like to see blood on the pitch'), I thought I might be on a sticky wicket in this very Australian shrine and expected a bit of banter from the museum staff – getting called 'you Pommy b******', perhaps – but I was welcomed warmly and even encouraged to have my photo taken, bat in hand, in front of a bust of that great Australian hero in the room where he was born.

Lunch was in the local park in the company of numerous rosella parrots displaying their gorgeous rainbow-coloured plumage as they foraged in the grass. Robert Hughes wrote wonderfully evocative descriptions of the parrots that new arrivals in the 18th century would have marvelled at. Cockatoos were 'raucous dandies... big birds with hoarse squalling voices, chalk-white plumage... and an insouciant lick of yellow feathers curling back from the head. When excited, they would flirt their crests erect into nimbi of golden spikes like Aztec headdresses'. And galah parrots had 'fronts of the most delicate, intense dusty pink, like the center of a Bourbon rose', and uttered 'small grating cries like the creak of rusty hinges'. But of course cockatoos and galahs are still around, and we saw many of them perched up in the gum trees. In Sydney parks we had also seen ibis, as common as pigeons back home except they're like a fat heron with a lethal six-inch curved beak, and a scavenging habit that has earned them the nickname 'bin chickens'.

North of Cootamundra we stopped briefly at Wombat (pop. 120) to buy some delicious cherries and strawberries at the roadside. Our final stop that day was at Cowra, famous for an incident at the town's POW camp during World War II – the Cowra Breakout. One night in 1944 over 1000 Japanese prisoners stormed the fences, to the surprise of the Australian guards who scrambled to man a couple of machine guns. By morning, 200 or so prisoners had been killed, but hundreds more had escaped (most were subsequently captured). To the Japanese, imprisonment was a disgrace, and the only honourable thing to do was to escape or die in the attempt. By contrast, Italian prisoners at the camp had been glad to get away from the desert war in North Africa and were quite content with life at Cowra, even being trusted to work without supervision on local farms. In their spare time they would hang out in town and flirt with women. Nothing now remains of the camp apart from some signage and the foundations of huts in a field. I'd wanted to walk across to look at the ruins, but some rather large kangaroos were lounging there in the late afternoon sunshine. I had no idea how a mob of 'roos in the wild might behave if I approached them, so I decided my time would be better spent checking emails back at the hotel.

Days 19-20

The last stage of our circular route: a damp day in Katoomba, the Gem of the Blue Mountains. At Echo Point we peered at The Three Sisters rock formation through an initial screen of drizzle but then as the mist cleared, endless eucalyptus forests were revealed stretching out to the horizon. After the photo reenactment with Mrs V, it was back to Sydney to retrieve our cases from storage, return the rental car, and head by taxi to Circular Quay to meet our next ship.

My feeling about Australia, as a first-timer, was that Ilsa Sharp, author of *Culture Shock! Australia*, got it exactly right:

So never be afraid to greet an Aussie in the street or to talk to a taxi-driver; always take the initiative if you can, because you will inevitably be rewarded with a smile and friendly conversation.

This advice does sound suspiciously like the kind of thing you say to a gullible foreigner for a laugh, though ('When visiting the Scottish Highlands be sure to tell your hosts that it's your favourite part of England.'). But from our limited experience – we're British, so we couldn't just go round greeting complete strangers, could we? – the natives had indeed been friendly. Informal, too. They love to shorten words, and we saw plenty of examples: *stubbies* (bottles of beer), *tinnies* (cans of beer), *schoolies* (children, or school holidays), *workies* (workmen), *fisho* (fisherman), *pokies* (slot machines), *salties* (saltwater crocodiles) and *dimmies* (dim sim dumplings). Mild swear words are common, and not only in speech: Tourism Australia's slogan for an international ad campaign a few years ago was 'So where the bloody hell are ya?'

Then there's that word *pom*, or *pommy*, still a favourite term for a Brit though we weren't subjected to it, at least not in our hearing. Also popular, for some unknown reason, is the variation *whingeing pom* (we don't whinge, it's not true, that's so unfair!). The late, great Barry Humphries once joked that his wife was a secret drinker, and 'some nights she's as full as a Pommy Complaints Box'.

And now I will hand back over to She Who Must Be Obeyed.

NEW ZEALAND

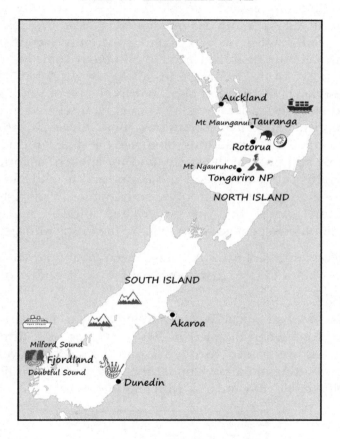

We had been as far as we could in Australia in the time allowing (without flying) and loved it all: the changing scenery – from coast, to farmland, to bush – and the constant surprise of new flowers and birds that we had never seen before, or at least that I could recall. The gum trees, which thrive in every type of Australian climate, whether bush or snow, the calls of the kookaburras and parrots, the beguiling Aboriginal names – Jindyandy, Parramatta, Murrumbidgee – made indelible impressions. People were jokey, friendly and helpful, as Mr Verne has mentioned. Most didn't realise we were English, as our accent apparently blended in with certain Australian accents, although someone did think we were from as far afield as Adelaide. The lifestyle, at first glance, appeared to be one of sand, sea and stubbies, at least for the young, who seemed in the majority. Our only reservations about lovely Australia concerned the ubiquitous fondness for piped music in shops and even in the street, and for spoken 'historical' narrative in galleries and museums; and a tendency to wrong usage of apostrophes and commas, not just in grocery stores but on public and official signage. Naturally we penned a stiff letter to the Prime Minister.

How different would I have been had I grown up here? Hard to say. I just know that I loved it, and want to return.

But we had a boat to catch, sailing away as my parents had done when they left in 1961 – forever, as it turned out. As we passed Kirribilli I said a final goodbye to them, sitting in the park under the bridge with their little girls, bewildered and sick with longing for home.

Our new ship was the *Celebrity Solstice*, a sleek white giant with a passenger capacity not far shy of 3,000, all of whom were seemingly on board. We had good accommodation with a verandah (the same as a balcony, but it sounds posher), though the cabin was a tight squeeze for all our luggage. Irritatingly, there was no guest laundry. Security was excellent, however, as they found and confiscated the tiny fruit knife we'd been planning to stab people with. They also confiscated the bottle of whisky we'd concealed beneath layers of clothing in a suitcase, as of course any X-ray machine worth its salt would have detected it immediately. We were allowed to retrieve it on disembarkation in New Zealand, Mr Verne making the walk of shame along with several other hangdog miscreants.

It was certainly a busy ship. The buffet was the usual zoo, and there were long waits for the crowded lifts. I think we must have mortally offended our initial dinner companions in some way because after the first night they never came back (hardly surprising, you might well be thinking), but luckily they were replaced by a very pleasant couple who managed to put up with us.

Formal nights on Celebrity ships were now something called Evening Chic: dressier than Smart Casual, but less dressy than Formal. But you could dress formal if you wanted to. Celebrity must have known this vague policy would cause trouble because in some corporate guidance we found on the internet they advise staff how to answer the following very reasonable question (or rather, how to avoid answering it):

Guest: I don't want to be in the dining room in a tuxedo or gown, and sit next to someone in jeans.

Staff answer: I can understand that. The beauty of Evening Chic is that guests who wish to wear traditional formal wear can still do so, and guests who wish to dress up in a nice pair of jeans, or wear their favorite little black dress can do so, too.

South Island

According to Maori legend, the demigod Maui sailed from Hawaiki (believed to be one of the French Polynesian islands) in his canoe, and he caught a huge fish, which he dragged to the surface. The fish is the North Island; Maui's canoe is the South Island.

(Fodor's *Essential New Zealand*)

There was a relaxing day at sea before chugging into the first of the famous fjords, or 'sounds', as they are termed in New Zealand. Rain and fog was the order of the day in Milford Sound, unfortunately, so views were mainly of the very steep, sometimes vertical sides and just glimpses of mountain up above. At least we saw some seals on a rock, but so far away they were the size of slugs. Some of the passengers were landed for a tour and afterwards the *Solstice* gently manoeuvred around to exit the sound the same way it had entered. The weather slowly worsened as we headed on to Doubtful Sound, so named by Captain Cook because he was not sure he would be able to get out if he went in, and chose not to take the risk. Strong winds were even making some of the waterfalls blow right back up the way they had come, and the rain and fog grew ever denser. The

Captain sensibly cancelled the scheduled sail up Dusky Sound.

Next morning the *Solstice* pulled up at Port Chalmers on South Island for a look at Dunedin, a city known for both its Maori and Scots heritage. In fact the name comes from the Gaelic word for Scotland's capital, and the city was originally intended to be a new Edinburgh. Perhaps more in spirit than actuality. Despite spotting a Princes St, a statue of poet Robert Burns, and even a bus to Corstorphine, Edinburgh it ain't – more like Basildon town centre on a February afternoon (no disrespect to one of the UK's finest towns). The suburbs were very pleasant though, with Scottish-type houses, and the surrounding hills were an astonishing green. We left the city for a walk up Baldwin St in the suburbs, once cited in the Guinness Book of Records as the steepest street in the world. Peering up from the bottom of Baldwin St I could see it *looked* a bit steep further up, but it seemed perfectly doable. We knew there was a yearly run up and down it, the Baldwin Street Gutbuster – how bad could it be? Very bad, as it turned out. The hill quickly became what you could only call downright perpendicular, and only about a quarter of the way up I was on my hands and knees, gasping and clutching at hedges to keep my balance; meanwhile, cars full of screaming teenagers raced up and down beside us in what appeared to be the local way of passing the time. To me, going up in a vehicle would have been infinitely worse because of my fear of sliding backwards. Intrepid Mr Verne ventured out into the middle of the road with his camera but I quickly gave up and lurched back down, which was even harder than climbing up. (Meanwhile, possibly the world's fittest postman was totally at his ease.)

A woman waiting with us at the bus stop told us that tourists were generally welcomed in the area, just not the ones who walked breezily into their gardens to take photos. Understandable that some did, though – there were some really wonderful displays of flowers in those gardens, especially roses.

We sailed away in now beautiful weather, the sun shining down on the curving coastline of the inlet and surrounding hills as people stopped in their cars to gaze at the departing ship. Others lounged or fished on the beaches. Dressed in warm clothes.

Our next stop along the coast, Akaroa, was a very pretty seaside village at the end of an inlet and at the centre of an extinct volcano, the extravagant floral arrays in many of the cottage gardens far outdoing old Dunedin.

There was a tender to get ashore, after which we felt we deserved a cup of good coffee (luckily finding it), and Mr Verne also plunged headfirst into a 'brekkie pie', the local version of an egg and bacon quiche. Thus refreshed we set out to explore, and soon noticed some surprising street names like Rue Jolie and Rue Lavaud and a guesthouse flying the French tricolour. This Gallic influence apparently dates from when a French ship carrying a few dozen hopeful settlers arrived in 1840 and found that the British had got there first and claimed the land, but seeing as the French had come such an awfully long way the British did the decent thing and let them have their own little settlement in the bay.

Wanting to escape from all the cruise ship passengers in this tiny place, we then took the always dodgy step of going for a ramble, knowing full well that at some point there would be a moment of panic on finding ourselves looking down at the tiny ship from the top of a mountain ten miles away. After a stretch of 'bush' – far more benign, and less alien, than Australian bush – and a bit of climbing, we stopped at a farmhouse for a break. Here the very kind owner made us extremely welcome with a free drink of lemon herb water and permission to eat our packed lunch on a verandah overlooking a garden of exotic wild flowers, and even to read his Sunday paper as we did so. He refused any payment. Mind you, the house and verandah were strewn with cushions and throws in a profusion of rich red and purple velvets suggestive of a 19th-century French bordello, and I did wonder if we were being drugged prior to a one-way trip to the basement to await his pleasure, but he must have decided to let us go. Too old.

We reached a high point with fabulous views of the surrounding hills and green, green countryside in brilliant sunshine, then ran back down. Made it to the tender on time, thank goodness.

After our Akaroa ramble, a day at sea was for us a day of rest. What better way to relax than with a nice cuppa? Not if you're on the *Solstice*. As usual with American-owned ships, the quality of tea on board was, let's say, indifferent, and we were sorely tempted to deploy a favourite old *Punch* joke: 'Look here, steward, if this is coffee I want tea; but if this is tea, I want coffee.' Having travelled a lot in the US we suspect they actually know how to make a perfectly good cup of tea, but for British customers, instead of pouring boiling water *onto* the loose tea or teabag to release the flavour (as divinely ordained), they reach for a giant cardboard cup, fill it with lukewarm water and plonk a tea bag of the weakest variety on the side, then pretend not to understand when you ask for milk. Is all this in retaliation for us torching their White House in 1814? Conversely, a US work colleague used to have a theory that we British put on our effete accent while in public but speak pure American between ourselves at home. (It's true, actually.)

Up on the highest deck we found the Lawn Club, which unusually for a cruise ship is an expanse of real grass. Actually, according to Celebrity, it's an 'expanse of pure innovation... brought to life by a team of turf and soil scientists, irrigation specialists, and landscape architects... The refined setting is reminiscent of a country club'. But it really was just a bit of lawn, where you could practise your putting or enjoy a nice cup of weak, lukewarm 'tea'.

North Island

The ship docked at Tauranga, location of the smallish extinct volcano Mount Maunganui, a sacred Maori site that allowed public access. Every passenger (and most of the crew) duly climbed up it, encountering mist at the top and a good view of the shoreline below, lined with beautiful pohutukawa trees – famed for their bright red flowers in summer, and known as the Christmas trees of New Zealand. While hiking up the Mount we ran into a woman off the ship who told Mr Verne she had loved his magic show; not for the first time, my husband had been taken for one of the entertainers. It must be some kind of sleazy quality he has.

On the day of disembarkation in Auckland we and twenty or thirty other passengers also leaving the ship were forced to rise at five in the morning to be ready, with luggage, to meet immigration officers. With complete predictability we then sat pointlessly for a whole hour while just a handful of people were interviewed in another area, after which we all had our passports stamped and were free to stumble into breakfast. We finally left the ship at 9:30, having had our madly dangerous fruit knife returned to us by security.

At this point my every dream came true, for right there, in the bathroom of the studio apartment we had booked in Auckland, stood our very own washer and dryer. Delirious with joy after so many days without sight of a laundry, I got a load on and began the unpacking while Mr Verne sloped off with his camera. Too tired to do much else after our ridiculously early start, I spent the rest of the day relaxing and shopping for groceries – lovely to cook for ourselves, for once, and to eat meals without feeling obliged to supply sparkling conversation (admittedly a description our dinner companions on the *Solstice* might not have recognised). You can't sit there in dead silence, so new topics have to be continually found, which can be quite an effort and one not always made by everyone. In the end it always proves worthwhile, though. People get more and more interesting as they open up and you get to know them, of course, and there have been some fascinating revelations. Just not all the time.

Mr Verne, meanwhile, checked out an excellent collection of Maori artefacts at the Auckland Museum: carvings, war canoes, weapons, and a reconstructed tribal *marae* or meeting place that you could walk into, which is not normally permitted with the real thing. The top floor was a war museum highlighting New Zealand's contribution to various world conflicts, and Mr Verne hoped that the groups of Japanese and German tourists were suitably edified by the loud recordings of battles in the Pacific and Hitler's speeches following them around the room.

Our accommodation was not far from Parnell 'village', an attractive area of bijou shops, galleries, and cafés; nearby were quiet backstreets of pastel and white clapboard houses, their balconies hung with glorious flowers. Are all the historic parts of Australasian towns and cities so heartbreakingly pretty? But our stay in Auckland had to be short. The plan was to tour as much of North Island as we could by car, so we picked up our large rental, loaded up the suitcases full of lovely fresh washing, and set off to explore.

North of the city of Hamilton we found a scenic park on a river for a picnic in the warm sunshine. A group of Maori youngsters were playing around and diving into the water, clearly enjoying themselves, and so were we. A canoe-shaped sign outlined the significance of the river to the Maoris in times gone by – the first of many such informational signs about the 'history' of an area which, confusingly, offered Maori legend without any historical fact. Hamilton itself seemed mainly Maori, and we were to learn that the indigenous population (a full quarter of the whole) tend to live more in certain areas than in others. Generally, it seemed to be that Maori people and language have more of a presence than do Aboriginal peoples in Australia. The national coat of arms features a white female figure and a Maori chief, and on occasion we saw the name Aotearoa instead of New Zealand (pronounced aow-teya-RO-a, and meaning Land of the Long White Cloud). We heard Maori spoken on the streets, and discovered that kia ora is Maori for hello, not the name of a nasty type of orange juice as it was in our British childhoods.

Stopping later at a small town for a cold drink we were beguiled by the repeated syllables of its name, Kihikihi. Delightful place names like these derive from the grammatical rules of the Maori language but, contrary to what you might think, the effect of the doubling up (called reduplication) is to *reduce* the intensity of a meaning, rather than reinforce it: 'wera' means hot, but 'werawera' means warm. Other towns were more difficult to pronounce, all strangely similar and with lots of vowels, but the sound of the sung language at a couple of cultural performances later in the trip was arrestingly melodic.

Driving on we began to see traces of Scots heritage here too, including a couple of bagpipers in kilts practising outside a local library. We were headed for the volcanic area of Tongariro, where the *Lord of the Rings* movie trilogy was made. I thought we were going to be able to avoid it, but no.

> • **Mr Verne's fun facts:** Ever since the *LOTR* movies came out all those years ago, the New Zealand tourist board has been promoting the country as 'Home of Middle-earth'. Depressingly, the term Middle-earth and all other places, characters and events from the novel are now trademarked, giving lawyers (boo! hiss!) the chance to bully the little guy who is just trying to earn a crust and make us smile: in 2023 a two-man waste collection business in the UK called Lord of the Bins was ordered to change its name after being accused of breaching trademark laws. They were forced to ditch their company slogan as well – 'One ring to remove it all'. A cryptocurrency named 'JRR Token' was also

barred from operating. Although obviously meant as humorous, the digital token's name was deemed 'confusingly similar' to that of the *LOTR* author's. I suppose if you're dim enough to confuse the two you do need legal protection.

The landscape became bleaker and the sky cloudier as we came in sight of our hotel, the impressively named Chateau Tongariro, set against a brooding, misty, mountainous backdrop.

This was where the film crew had once stayed while shooting scenes in Tongariro National Park, using the hotel cinema to view daily footage. It was certainly atmospheric in the hotel, whose warren of dark and gloomy corridors was like something out of *The Shining*, the film that seems forever lodged in our memories. It became the base camp for my own personal expedition up Everest: a *sixteen*-km hike out to a crater lake that seemed to take several lifetimes.

Of course I was duped into going. Mr Verne knew full well there was no way I would agree to tackle the famous Tongariro Crossing – 18 km one-way – so instead he suggested a much more modest, circular stroll to a scenic waterfall (his eyes shifting from side to side as he did so). And he failed to mention that the visitor centre was predicting an increased likelihood of eruption and mudflows, so the advice was to cross rivers and valleys quickly. It started off like an enjoyable tramp (a New Zealand term) in Scotland: rolling hills and scrubby gorse, mists obscuring the uplands which slowly morphed into beech woods descending to a gorge heavy with moss and ferns. Taranaki Falls, when we reached it, was an impressive cataract crashing into a pool and throwing off clouds of spray – another perfect place for a picnic lunch in the sunshine.

'Why don't we press on to Lower Tama Lake?' came the oh so innocent suggestion from Mr Verne after this pleasant interlude.

I hadn't prepared for anything really strenuous and was wearing open-toed sandals rather than proper hiking boots (well all right, I don't own any). It's not much further, my husband swore. So off we set along a well marked and well maintained trail, which at first seemed reassuring, suggesting that people were back and forth all the time. The terrain gradually became more and more barren as we climbed, the views of the icy slopes of Mount Ruapehu and Mount Ngauruhoe (Mount Doom in *Lord of the Rings* movies) ever more spectacular.

Ancient lava flows carpeted with green, white and brown ferns and tiny colourful alpine flowers opened up before us but I rapidly lost interest as on and on we toiled, me in my inadequate footwear, up and down, up and down, breasting crest after crest only to discover another one beyond. It was endless. We asked a returning hiker (a pilgrim on the trail of *LOTR* film locations, no doubt) how much further to the lake.

'Oh, about half an hour,' he replied airily.

After about half an hour we asked the same question of another hiker.

'A good hour,' came the answer. As in some ghastly nightmare, the lake was getting *further away* the longer we walked.

Finally we arrived, but only for a short rest: we had to get all the way back before dark, and it had started to rain. (Wisely, Mr Verne did not suggest carrying on to *Upper* Tama Lake, a mere one and a half kilometres up a steep incline.) The crater lake was pretty and may well have been icy, but it was nothing to the marital atmosphere when after hours and hours and hours we staggered into the Chateau and threw ourselves onto the bed, every bone aching, feet red-hot and burning. Mr Verne, knowing the lie of the land, offered no resistance when I made him get up and go back out for fish and chips, our first sustenance since sandwiches at the falls several aeons ago.

Frosty conditions prevailed into next day, but at breakfast at least I had the satisfaction of observing some glum-looking hikers setting off in a steady drizzle, while we had a nice warm car ride ahead to the hot springs at Rotorua about a hundred miles away.

Rotorua

The designs are so flowing and graceful and beautiful… It takes but fifteen minutes to get reconciled to the tattooing… After that, the undecorated European face is unpleasant and ignoble.

(Mark Twain, *Following The Equator*)

● **Mr Verne's fun facts**: New Zealand ('Tattoo Land' in *Moby-Dick*) has a long tradition of flesh carving. Full face tattoos – usually on males – used to be cut into the skin with a knife or a chisel and mallet, while pigments were typically made from fish oil mixed with burnt caterpillar larvae or resin. Tattoos are still in fashion but modern needles and inks are now the norm.

As we drove along we started to see steam rising from random places in the countryside, and at Rotorua itself the smell of sulphur was hard to avoid. The very small, thin-walled rooms at the motel each had a pool at the back that could be filled with thermally heated water, but inside it stank of sulphur, and so did the whole town, all the time – obviously the price the poor locals had to pay for living by one of the natural wonders of the world. Perhaps they no longer noticed it.

Where we have *Keep off the grass* signs in our parks back home, Rotorua's say *Danger – thermal activity*. On the shore of Lake Rotorua, steam rose from the back gardens of several houses and we could see bubbling hot pools; we read that local residents often use the hot springs for cooking, heating their houses and bathing (temperature permitting).

> • **Mr Verne's fun facts (yet again):** When novelist Anthony Trollope swung by in 1872 he spent a pleasant evening in a pool with three very welcoming Maori damsels. A Captain Mair of the British Army acted as guide for Trollope and later recalled that the distinguished visitor discreetly omitted one little detail from his chronicles:
>
> "After we had been in the water some time, the old chap said, 'I wish I had something to lean against.' So I whispered to a fine young woman of splendid proportions... who immediately set her capacious back against his, whereat he exclaimed, 'Well, Mair. This is very delightful, don't you know; but I think I did wisely in leaving Mrs. Trollope in Auckland.'"

Two old geysers in Rotorua

We wandered around a small Maori settlement by the lake that was open to tourists, and admired the meeting hall with its characteristic carvings and decoration but, as is the custom, we were not allowed to enter without permission. We trod cautiously, though, as local people and pets have been known to disappear suddenly into boiling hot mud when a patch of fragile ground gave way beneath them. Nearby was an Anglican church, its interior unlike any we had ever seen: dark wood pews and pulpit were all elaborately carved Maori-style, there were woven textiles on the walls, and etched into a window was a large image of Jesus wearing a Maori feather cloak.

The following afternoon was spent in a 'geothermal wonderland' with the magnificent-sounding name of Te Whakarewarewatangaoteopetauaawahiao (shortened to Te Puia for the benefit of tourists), where a guided tour took in the natural curiosities of the area but also introduced visitors to aspects of Maori culture. First of all came a fascinating Maori welcoming ceremony, which started with a Maori warrior emerging from his *marae* brandishing a long wooden weapon at an enemy 'chief', a previously selected member of our group of tourists.

After a series of menacing waves of his spear and facial grimaces, he then placed a fern leaf on the ground as a peace gesture; our intrepid chief, having been told his moves in advance, walked slowly forward and picked it up. This launched the full welcoming ceremony, after which we were allowed to approach and enter the *marae*, but keeping well behind our chief. Inside came a performance of 'action songs' and the Poi dance, which featured women rhythmically swinging balls attached to flax strings, originally a way for them to keep their hands flexible for weaving and also, when the Poi was danced by men, to maintain the strength and coordination required during battle. The men then performed the ceremonial haka war dance, with all its foot stomping, tongue protrusion and rhythmic body slapping, accompanied by loud chanting. All of this seemed to us a spirited, joyful and proud demonstration of Maori culture that could only inspire respect – in strong contrast to a Maori performance on the *Solstice* a few days earlier, which had involved jokey audience participation that could only be described as demeaning. (The ships don't always get it wrong, though. Some of the cultural performances by the crew members themselves had been enchanting.)

We followed a path taking us past erupting geysers, bubbling mud pools, and glistening white rocks tinged with sulphurous yellow, then were led to the carving school where trainees were working on elaborate designs hewn out of giant logs. Our tour of Te Puia ended with a visit to the kiwi house, where in very dim lighting we could just make out the rear end of a sleeping bird. Kiwis being nocturnal and reclusive, I suppose we couldn't have expected much more. In 2023, though, a Miami zoo ruffled quite a few feathers when footage went viral of a kiwi bird being petted under bright lights by visitors who had paid $25 for a 'kiwi encounter'. After a flood of complaints from outraged New Zealanders about this mistreatment of their beloved national icon – it appears on coins and stamps, a famous fruit bears its name and, indeed, the natives call themselves 'Kiwis' – a chastened zoo spokesman admitted to a huge mistake: 'We have offended a nation.'

It was nearing Christmas and Rotorua was getting livelier, even if there was little in the way of decorations on the streets or houses. On the other hand, there was plenty of Christmas muzak in the shops and even sometimes in public toilets (most festive). Shopping was now the order of the day. Our very short exploration of this lush, beautiful, friendly country was almost at an end, and we began a desperate scurry for souvenirs and gifts; we had already bought a pair of possum and merino socks (no, really) as a present for a lucky someone, but more was needed. Far more importantly, we needed books to read on our upcoming voyage all the way across the Pacific to the United States. As in Australia, new books were extremely expensive, so it was sheer delight to come across an excellent secondhand shop. Emerging with about twelve books, we turned to tracking down that other elusive item, an electric travel kettle, but none seemed right and in the end we had to abandon the search. What we did buy was a cheap holdall for all the books, toiletries, food supplies and other myriad recently acquired stuff, so that our luggage now consisted of the following:

- three large suitcases
- three large holdalls
- one small overnight bag for souvenirs, and
- Mr Verne's gadget bag for electronics, cables, chargers, adaptors, cameras, etc. etc. etc.

When people advise travelling light, I can only give a hollow laugh. How, exactly? We simply can't do it.

Tauranga

Our final destination was again Tauranga, from where we would be setting sail on Christmas Day. Our B&B was immaculate and the room large and comfortable, with a walk-in closet – heavenly. Walk-in closets are unusual in Britain, where you have to wrestle your clothes out of a stuffed wardrobe and you can't see what's in there. At least here we could easily pick out some rainwear when, on Christmas Eve, we awoke to showers after a night of heavy rain (there's a reason for all that lushness). We were headed for a kiwi fruit farm up in a forest conservation area, which was also home to the shy and retiring kiwi bird. The hugely fertile volcanic soil supported all kinds of other fruit, the friendly guide told us on a buggy ride around the orchards, pointing out the tangelo trees and their delicious half-grapefuit, half-tangerine crop. Kiwi vines grew at a phenomenal rate and come harvest time some 25,000 people were employed, many of them backpackers. As the vines were less than six feet high, the rather tall Mr Verne was thrilled to be told he'd make a good tractor driver rather than picker, a job he had dreamt of since he was a boy. The bulk of the crop is the traditional green variety of kiwi (see below) but one quarter are golds – sweet and succulent, and a revelation if you've never tasted one, which we hadn't. Unfortunately, at the time we visited, disease was decimating the golds, so that trees were being cut back and new ones started by grafting golden shoots onto old green stumps. Already rare enough to see outside of New Zealand, there would now be even fewer golds exported to the rest of the world over the years to come.

Our B&B hosts were charming and hospitable, and on the evening of Christmas Day they very kindly threw a little drinks party for their guests, all of us far from home. Yes, instead of being out to sea as planned, we were still on dry land. Those of you still awake at this point may remember that we were booked to board a cargo boat – now delayed by a day – because there was no cruise ship leaving New Zealand at the right time for the United States, where we wanted to visit family again. We were stocking up on books and foodstuffs because, while every cruise ship has a library and lots of food, this is absolutely not the case on a freighter.

Christmas Day itself was spent mooching along the almost deserted beach, missing the normal chaos of the holiday and wondering how the family were managing. (There had been several frantic emails when it was finally understood we would not be home, indignantly asking who was going to cook the lunch.) Some other lonely souls eventually appeared, a few in swimwear and Santa hats. Our own dismal Christmas lunch was fish and chips (again), not even served on plates at the only café that was open, but later on we enjoyed the snacks and excellent New Zealand wine served at the B&B bash. As the drink flowed Mr Verne became quite morose thinking about the racks and racks of local Sauvignon Blancs we would be leaving behind at the supermarkets.

It was not just the wine we would miss, of course. People had been so kind and friendly, and the luxuriant country was a gorgeous mix of Scotland and the tropical colours of the Caribbean. Except for the confusion about apostrophes and love of muzak shared with Australia, we'd move there like a shot.

Crossing the Pacific by cargo boat

Where lies the land to which the ship would go?
Far, far ahead, is all her seamen know.
And where the land she travels from? Away,
Far, far behind, is all that they can say.

(Arthur Hugh Clough)

There is nothing so desperately monotonous as the sea, and
I no longer wonder at the cruelty of pirates.

(James Russell Lowell, *At Sea*)

As mentioned some time ago, it was not my first voyage on a cargo boat. When we went to work in America for a few years in our thirties, rather than fly I had actually sailed there on a cargo boat with our two young sons, with Mr Verne meeting us in Baltimore after taking a flight a week or so before. The littlest was only five, so you can imagine how anxious I was at first about his safety – in fact now I don't know what on earth I was thinking. In the event, most of the day was spent inside because there was very little deck space, and it was mostly terrible weather anyway. The crew, away from their own families for months on end, made a great fuss of the boys for the entire trip and they had a whale of a time – the Italian captain once even turned the boat right around in a giant circle in the middle of the ocean just to amuse them. We were accommodated in the owner's relatively palatial suite (not with the owner, I hasten to add, he wasn't on board) and there were several other passengers for adult company. The usual cruise ship activities and services were of course absent, but we made our own fun and we all enjoyed it. I remembered the voyage very fondly. 'It will be wonderful!' I burbled to Mr Verne about the upcoming trip.

The *Matisse* was the usual type of freighter: a bit battered-looking, a long, long deck at the front piled high with huge containers, and at the back a turret of living areas, offices, and the bridge. Boarding was up a steep ramp, rather than the usual gently inclining gangway onto a cruise ship, but at least we were spared the lengthy processing before being able to get on: the shipping agent drove us straight to the ship from the port gate. Once aboard, we were asked to remain in the saloon to meet the Romanian captain and be interviewed by an immigration official – a mere formality, it appeared, as our bags weren't even checked. Then we were taken to our cabin.

Not an owner's suite this time, but big enough – in fact larger than many a cruise ship cabin – with its own bathroom of course, and the usual fittings, if not exactly luxurious: bed, wardrobe, desk, chair, sofa, fridge. Our porthole faced the prow across the stretch of colourful containers, and could be opened, unlike most present-day cruise ships. The largish passenger saloon was available for tea and coffee-making and DVD watching, and there was even a tiny outside area a little way up the corridor where we could sit and watch the endless Pacific sliding by. A couple of decks down was a games room with a small library and some gym equipment, and directly opposite the cabin, you will be pleased to hear, was a little room with a washing machine in it which we seemed to have to ourselves. What am I saying. *I* had the washer to *myself*. Mr Verne never went near it.

We had a front-row seat as giant containers glided past our window and were lowered smoothly and accurately into the hold. It was mesmerising.

Mr Verne tells me that the history of the standardised shipping container is fascinating, and really it's such a shame that we don't have space here to include the fruits of his detailed research. In any case, our cargo on this trip was unknown to us, but in the era of globalisation you can imagine the random nature of the items being transported. And the way countries swap goods is bizarrely inefficient, as a crew member revealed to Horatio Clare in his book *Down to the Sea in Ships:* 'We take our milk and cheese to Montreal, and bring their milk and cheese back... We take Philips and Grundig and Bang & Olufsen to the East and bring Sony and Hitachi back.'

Our first night aboard felt remarkably smooth. This cargo ship is wonderful, we were thinking, but next morning when we opened our curtains there was Mount Maunganui still framed by our porthole. We hadn't moved. The *Matisse* did finally set sail after breakfast on the 27th, and as we headed out to sea we came abeam of White Island, an active volcano, where guided tours were discontinued in 2019 after a violent eruption killed 22 people out of the 47 present on the island.

At lunchtime back on that first day in dock we had headed to the mess to meet the other passengers in a state of some trepidation. Naturally you are far more thrown together in a cargo ship, and getting along is crucial. There's no escape, either at meals or when trying to occupy yourself, except by retreating to your cabin.

Seated at the passenger table was a solitary man about a decade older than ourselves. That was it. We quickly established that he was the only other passenger on the ship, and that we would be sharing the saloon and dining table with just him for the next three weeks. Let's call him Bill. At lunch he told us all about himself: a Brit like us, he was a widower who had spent most of his adult life in Adelaide, where he had embarked. Having retired, Bill was now heading back to Britain for the first time since leaving forty-five years previously.

Over those three weeks – long, long weeks – we found out a lot about Adelaide but Bill never found out anything about us, not where we came from, or worked, or had travelled to, because he never asked. Not a single question. If we did offer any remarks about ourselves, Bill would make absolutely no comment or show the slightest interest, but instead relate it in some way to Adelaide: 'Oh, we never do that in Adelaide,' or 'The trains in *Adelaide* always run on time,' etc. etc. It became a game between Mr Verne and myself to see who could come out with the most startling statement, just to watch Bill being completely uninterested and find a way to relate it to a certain city in South Australia. He was an odd character, possibly with some kind of psychological condition or even early dementia, and we began to feel a little concerned that he was travelling so far and for so long on his own. Later, at the various ports of call, Bill attached himself to us like a leech and all our excursions had to be in his company, despite our increasing desperation. We just had to live with it, and in the end we even became quite fond of him, like a slightly dotty relative that you accept and even enjoy because of the dottiness.

We settled down to a routine. Breakfast was from 7 to 8 am (with Bill), followed by lunch at 12 (with Bill), and then dinner at 7 (with Bill). On my previous cargo boat odyssey with the children all the passengers had shared one big table with the ship's officers, but on the *Matisse* passengers ate separately at a little table away from the crew's, where Mr Verne and I listened sourly to the captain and crew laughing and talking in Romanian and having a good time. There was no buffet and no menu: they just dished up whatever it was, and of course there was no room service in the cabin. You either turned up in the mess at the right time or went hungry. Lunch and dinner came with wine – a cheap Spanish tinto – and the food was reasonable. At first.

We were always free to visit the bridge, and Mr Verne soon made a habit of going up to check the Captain was doing it right.

*Mr Verne, Master and Commander of the
Matisse*

Otherwise we read, either inside or out on our private 'deck', wrote up our journals and blog, sorted photographs, napped (a lot), ate, went on the treadmill in the games room, and worked through the stock of DVDs in the evenings. With Bill. Occasionally we might go and check emails in the communications room, the only place with internet access. After a while I began to notice, as I moved around the small area we had access to, that while the ship's officers greeted me politely, the members of the crew who did the real work out on the open decks tended to avoid my eye. Mr Verne suggested that as these men were at sea for years at a time, they might not be able to restrain themselves in the face of my extreme attractiveness. I could only agree (and award him the several brownie points he had been looking for).

This routine was not very much different from the way we occupied our time on cruise ships – except for the limited company at meals. The days were all very similar, and two of them were not only similar but actually identical: we had the first Friday on the ship twice, for various complicated reasons few really comprehend – my head spins when I try to understand exactly why, but I know at least that we got back the day we had lost on our way to Japan three months before.

In Jules Verne's *Around the World in 80 Days* novel, Phileas Fogg famously arrived back in London thinking he was a day too late and had therefore lost the £20,000 bet, but he soon discovered that it was actually a day earlier and so he was able to claim his prize. For the benefit of his readers Verne explained that Fogg miscalculated because he hadn't known to jump back 24 hours when crossing the Pacific eastwards, a concept unfamiliar to many landlubbers until the International Date Line was introduced in 1884, eleven years after publication of the novel.

For his *Around the World in 80 Days* TV series, British actor and comedian Michael Palin took a cargo ship from Tokyo to LA, and described how as they were about to cross the Date Line the captain announced over the tannoy, 'We will have another Monday tomorrow. However, please don't expect whatever happened today will happen again tomorrow. Thank you.' (On the evening of our second Friday we marked this weird duplication by watching *Groundhog Day*. Bill didn't get this jokey choice on our part as he had never seen the movie in the first place.)

Our progress across the vast Pacific was naturally slow. Charles Darwin thought that long ocean voyages were tedious, a 'desert of water', though he acknowledged there were some delights – a moonlit night, a soft breeze filling the sails – between the long stretches of monotony. Our nighttime skies were filled with stars, more than we'd ever seen; who knew how romantic it could be standing at the rail of a cargo ship? But by day there were no other ships nor any kind of wildlife to relieve the monotony for the first twelve days after leaving Tauranga. It felt quite exciting when we were just (relatively) *near* something, as when the ship passed 200 miles south of Pitcairn Island (of *Mutiny on The Bounty* fame). We imagined what it must be like to visit that remote rocky outcrop, with its total population of about fifty, many of whom are descended from the *HMS Bounty* mutineers who landed there in 1790. In fact ten or so cruise ships do stop by each year, although they have to anchor offshore while islanders come out in longboats and climb aboard with souvenir carvings, T-shirts, baskets, jewellery, and pots of their famous honey made from mango, passion flower and guava nectar. One or two also give a talk about life on the island. In return, the islanders are given much-prized provisions such as beer and ice cream. The romance of it all fades somewhat when you learn that many of the islanders' products are now available to order online, but remember this is not Amazon, and the message about delivery time may surprise you: 'the mail ship is departing in 73 days' is normal.

Unfortunately for us, there was no way a cargo ship would stop at Pitcairn Island, and indeed we regretted that the *Matisse* was not going to dock at any of the fabled Pacific islands.

On and on we went. In hindsight, we were lucky not to have any bad seas, and it seems we just put out of our minds any thoughts of poor weather or accidents while being many hundreds of miles from land. Apart from early on in our passage to Japan, there had been remarkably few rough days overall. Do you suffer from seasickness? If not, you obviously have sea legs to be envied, possibly due to Viking ancestry. You can skip this section. The rest of you, read on.

Most people susceptible to *mal de mer* know to book a cabin mid-ships and on a lower deck, and if symptoms appear, to head out for some fresh air and watch the horizon. They may also be familiar with the usual tips for prevention or relief:

- tablets of Meclizine or Dramamine
- skin patch
- ginger, in tea or pill form
- dry crackers, green apples
- acupressure wristband
- 'mindfulness' and meditation

Some would add alcohol to that list. Whether you succumb or not, it's a great ice-breaker at dinner:

For the first two nights, who's feeling seasick and who's not and who's not now but was a little while ago or isn't feeling it yet but thinks it's maybe coming on, etc., is a big topic of conversation at Table 64 in the Five-Star Caravelle Restaurant. Discussing nausea and vomiting while eating intricately prepared gourmet foods doesn't seem to bother anybody.

(David Foster Wallace, *Harpers* magazine)

But none of that on our cargo ship, luckily. Instead, we simply enjoyed the fine, sunny days on our little square of deck as the *Matisse* ploughed valiantly on through a gently rolling seascape. Or, as Herman Melville put it more poetically and using some good old-fashioned sexist imagery in *Moby-Dick*:

It was a clear steel-blue day. The firmaments of air and sea were hardly separable in that all-pervading azure; only, the pensive air was transparently pure and soft, with a woman's look, and the robust and man-like sea heaved with long, strong, lingering swells, as Samson's chest in his sleep.

After twelve days at sea we finally glimpsed two seabirds (probably boobies) and some small flying fish, and more birds started following the ship once we had crossed the Equator. A lone sighting of dolphins was positively electrifying.

The Panama Canal and Colón

Approaching the Panama Canal in the late afternoon of the fifteenth day we saw land for the first time since leaving New Zealand. The *Matisse* parked some way off the entrance to the Canal, the skyscrapers of Panama City visible in the distance, as she waited her turn behind about thirty-three other vessels. We were anxious to get through quickly in order to have some promised time ashore at the other end, if possible, as the food situation was getting perilous. Our hoard of nuts and chocolate had run out, and we were clearly no longer aboard the *Queen Mary 2*: the ship itself had run out of basic items like butter and fruit; we were almost certainly approaching the explorer Magellan's situation in the 1500s, when he spent three months in the Pacific without any fresh food and his men had to resort to wormy biscuits, sawdust, rats, mast leather and putrid yellow water. We started through the canal at about five in the morning and made good progress.

Then, suddenly, we passed Holland America's *Prinsendam*, the ship we had sailed on to Antarctica in our first book, heading in the other direction. We waved madly, but could see no one waving back. However, incredibly, we *had* been spotted, by two old friends who were sailing again on the ship and thought they recognised my bright pink skirt. They emailed to ask if it was us.

> • **Mr Verne's very last fun fact:** A huge Panama Canal expansion project was completed a few years ago in order to handle the mega ships that are now common. It doubled the canal's capacity by adding deeper channels and two locks parallel to the old ones. The new locks are less fun, though, as tugboats are used instead of the cute little locomotives – 'mules' – that run on rails right next to the ship, ringing bells and flashing lights to communicate with the pilot. If you

go through the Panama Canal on one of the larger cruise ships, such as the *Norwegian Joy, Celebrity Edge, Caribbean Princess, Emerald Princess, Ruby Princess, Carnival Freedom,* or *Carnival Glory,* you will be going through the new locks. But a few mega cruise ships such as Royal Caribbean's *Symphony of the Sea*s or *Harmony of the Seas* are still too large for the canal, being wider than even the new locks or too tall to fit under the Bridge of the Americas at the Pacific end.

It was not our first sailing through the Panama Canal, but the experience of rising and falling in the various (old) locks was still amazing. On this occasion Mr Verne was allowed to be on the bridge, observing first-hand how the pilot issued his instructions – port 10, midships, stop engines – all the while maintaining communication with the shore by radio. We did get a few waves from people in the public gallery at Gatún locks, who might have been a little puzzled by the crew member wearing a pink skirt.

Fortunately we made good progress and were able to dock on the Atlantic side at Manzanillo International Terminal, where we dashed off the ship (with Bill) for the first time in over two weeks – dodging, on foot, a lot of cranes and forklifts and giant dangling hooks to reach the port exit. Passengers on cargo boats are not a priority, and in a busy port you have to take your chance.

The local shops were not too impressive, so after downing a very welcome fresh fruit smoothie we all got in a taxi for a drive around nearby Colón (Spanish for Columbus). According to one Panama guidebook, this was a highly risky move:

Sadly, there is no shortage of horror stories about Colón... Decades of neglect have left swathes of the city in disrepair, riddled with violence and crime, its population terminally deprived and marginalized... for now, it is assuredly off the tourist trail... Colón is not for the faint of heart.

Well, the colonial buildings in the old town there were stunning, with pretty balconies and colonnaded porticos, and families were enjoying themselves in a shaded park area along the main street. But the city was evidently extremely poor, so decrepit and shabby in places that we would have been nervous about walking there on our own, despite the presence of soldiers every few blocks.

The taxi driver told us that parts of Colón were to be rebuilt in order to transform the city into a 'free zone', or duty-free area, with the current residents scheduled to be moved out to new housing elsewhere. He was full of praise for Panama's then president, who was taking steps to alleviate his country's desperate poverty. Not everybody seemed to agree: we saw graffiti accusing the president of being a murderer and liable to 'sell your mother'.

'I hope they don't knock down these beautiful old buildings,' I remarked.

'Parts of Adelaide have been restored,' said Bill helpfully.

Having stocked up in a supermarket we hurried back to the *Matisse* – this was one ship that definitely wouldn't be waiting. In the cabin we emptied out our bags of chocolate and snacks, happy in the knowledge that the ship too would now have more food and we could look forward to better meals. Not so. For reasons not clear to us there had been no restocking whatsoever, and there wouldn't be until Savannah, where we were due to get off. Back to butterless breakfasts (with Bill).

JAMAICA: Kingston

Two days later we reached Kingston in Jamaica, hot in the sun but pleasant due to occasional cloudiness and a nice breeze. The shipping agent had arranged for us to be picked up by a local driver, Clovis, to see the sights. These included Emancipation Park, a neatly kept sweep of green dotted with lovely orchids and bougainvillea and graced by a startling sculpture of two giant, very naked Jamaicans, male and female, which I can assure you were anatomically correct in every respect (as we walked around it several times to check).

'We have a statue like that in Adelaide,' said Bill.

I don't think so.

After a delicious butter almond ice cream in the sunny grounds of Devon House, the first black-owned plantation, Clovis took us to where we really wanted to go: the Bob Marley Museum. It was closed, to our intense disappointment. So monotonous and alike were our days aboard ship, we had forgotten it was Sunday. As Mr Verne was crouching to take photos through the gate, a very laid-back local emerged to say he would let us into the front yard for some better photos, 'for a donation', which we duly coughed up.

As we drove away Clovis told us about the 'Marley Coffee' brand – slogan: 'Stir it Up' – and that Bob's music was taught in the schools and had been the subject of Clovis' college thesis. On to Clovis' favourite fast food joint for jerk chicken, pumpkin rice, and a sweet fried cornmeal dough called 'Festival', with a Ting grapefruit soda to wash it all down. Our tour ended with a drive through areas of Trenchtown worryingly called the 'Ghetto' and the 'Concrete Jungle' – rather a quick drive, which was fine by us. It was Clovis' idea and, as always, we felt very uncomfortable staring at people as though in a zoo.

However, despite the locked car doors as we sprinted through Trenchtown, and previous dire warnings from some of the ship's crew, there had been no problems whatsoever. People seemed friendly and relaxed, and we enjoyed the bright colours of the houses, the food, and the constant reggae everywhere we went. Kingston on this very brief acquaintance had felt safe and not at all hostile, although Clovis commented that things could be different on a weekday. In his view, corruption was rife, and there were terrible problems: poverty, crime, and continued neglect of the many homeless children on the streets. As far as he was concerned Jamaica's independence in 1962 had come too early and there was still much suffering all these decades later, even with aid arriving from abroad. He was a nice man, and gave us some CDs of contemporary reggae as a goodbye present.

The final stretch. Although the *Matisse* was going on all the way to the UK, we had decided to disembark in Savannah, Georgia, for a chance to see our eldest son and his family up in Baltimore. (After a second period we spent working in the US he had decided to go to college there, and just never came back. Now, you wouldn't even know he was English. We miss him, but our consolation is a lovely daughter-in-law and our wonderful American grandson.) Bill, as mentioned, was going to the end of the line to visit his British homeland, and, although after three weeks of his non-stop company we had got used to his strangeness, I think we might have had to hang ourselves had we stayed aboard any longer. In fact, when US immigration came aboard on docking, I became very anxious that we might be denied entry for unfathomable reasons and be forced to carry on. Fortunately the official said we could remain six months, and even request a longer stay if we needed it. Good old US of A. (When Michael Palin arrived in LA the customs officer joked: 'You're clear for customs. Enjoy your time in the US. Don't drink the water or eat the food.' My own favourite example of dry American wit came a few years earlier from a tour guide in Key West: 'I've checked out this gift shop for you, and it's a good one – they don't have security cameras.')

Reader, we thought we were more or less at the end of our epic journey, but suddenly we had word that a tenant had been found for our house in the UK, and the extra income enabled us to extend our stay in the US. After some months there seeing family, and old friends from working days who managed to look delighted that we had turned up again, we eventually took sail for Southampton aboard the dear old *Queen Mary 2*.

Queen Mary 2 (again)

The quayside porter in Brooklyn who came forward to take our bags was clutching a wad of dollar bills as a not-so-subtle hint. We were then stopped from entering the terminal because Mr Verne had unaccountably failed to print one of the several tickets required, and when he tried to suggest to the uniformed American official that surely one ticket was enough for both of us she barked 'I'm not gonna tell you a second time, sir,' at which point we checked to see if she was armed (she wasn't). She let us through anyway, but made sure we knew she was doing us a great favour, although anyone dealing with a constant stream of incompetents like Mr Verne might be forgiven a moment of testiness.

Don't tell Cunard but we smuggled aboard some whisky, this time in two Gatorade bottles innocently stowed on full view in the side pockets of Mr Verne's backpack. When we later told our son about this clever ruse he immediately pointed out that Gatorade didn't make any flavour that was the colour of whisky. We got away with it, though.

After so much exotic, expensive travel we had needed to go for the cheapest accommodation, and were in a rather small and claustrophobic inside cabin that never saw the light of day – a strange experience. Waking up in a windowed space is usually about being roused by the sun's rays creeping around the edge of curtains, but this was like sleeping underground: total blackness. You wake only from the sound of the alarm, and have no sense of the passage of time, which is very disorienting.

After a week of this, arrival in a sunny Southampton would later prove extremely welcome. As for the size of the cabin, it was better than the sardine can of an Amtrak sleeper but still *bijou* (a French term meaning cramped).

I say let the world go to pot so long as I always get my tea.

(Dostoyevsky, *Notes from Underground*)

We settled into the familiar, comfortable routines of life on board *QM2*, as described earlier in the outward journey from Southampton.

Serious walkers (not us)

One important Cunard ritual still needs to be addressed, though: afternoon tea in the Queens Room. Here is our insider guide to this very popular daily event. Queue early to bag a front row table for a prime view of the string quartet and for people watching, but also to be in pole position to drink as much proper British tea as you can – in our case, a lot – and wolf down those dainty sandwiches, scones and pastries as your very own contribution to the 700 scones and 6,000 cups of tea that are consumed per day aboard *QM2*. The quartet or harpist helps to distract you while you wait feverishly for the tables to fill up until, finally, the ritual begins and waiters fan out across the room bearing silver pots of freshly brewed tea and a great deal of carbohydrate. Your tea will have been made for you in the correct way, of course, with boiling – not merely hot – water, poured onto loose-leaf tea in a pre-warmed teapot. Add milk and sugar to taste – no honey on offer, this is a British ship. Scones are served with jam and cream but the nation is rancorously divided as to which goes on first, not that it matters in the slightest (except that jam on top of cream is just weird).

Tea over, you reel back to your cabin to lie down and wait for dinner, or there is plenty of space in public areas to find corners to relax in. Consider this: Royal Caribbean's *Freedom of the Seas* is about the same length and tonnage as *QM2*, but carries 2,000 more passengers.

One day, to while away some time, we revisited a couple of favourite haunts: the galleries. The photo gallery was an immediate disappointment – no photos taken by the *QM2* photographers were on display, but were accessible on a computer screen if you entered the relevant stateroom number. We had none of our own to view as we usually avoid being snapped, so we tried entering a few random numbers; nothing interesting came up and the staff seemed to grow suspicious. This new policy will annoy both the show-offs who want to be seen, and people like us who want to be entertained.

On, then, to the art gallery, which as usual had a few big names on display. Mr Verne noted prices and researched online later, leading him to the perhaps unsurprising conclusion that buying art at sea might not be the best value. A Picasso print priced at $36,000 was one of 300 made, but he discovered that several of those 300 had sold on dry land for less than $10,000 each. And a signed LS Lowry print of an industrial scene was on sale for $16,000, whereas others from the same set had sold at auction houses for less than $5,000. Lucky we didn't buy one, then. We never do anyway, as we know everything about art but we don't know what we like.

According to travel experts Frommer's, 'the Cunard of today is not the Cunard of yesterday, but then again, it is'. Well, that's clear, then. What they mean is that while Cunard is no longer one of the most dominant players, it still has old-world formality (good) and 'blatant class structure' (bad, unless you're the ones in a suite). And: 'Cunard attracts a well-traveled crowd of passengers mostly in their 50s and up, many of them repeaters who appreciate the line's old-timey virtues and are more the 4-o'clock-tea crowd than the hot-tub-and-umbrella-drink set.' Agreed. Unfortunately, this retro image projected by Cunard, and happily accepted by passengers and industry experts, perpetuates a weird British stereotype. To give just a couple of examples, Frommer's admire how 'crewmembers exhibit a polished sort of British demeanor', and an American passenger commented online that at dinner dishes are cleared 'in the English way' (we have no idea what this means – stacked in the sink for several days, maybe?). Mystifyingly, there is also the belief that 'the British love to iron everything, including their underwear'. Hardly.

From the hype you would think *QM2* is a cross between *Downton Abbey* and *The Crown,* possibly with a spoonful of *Mary Poppins* because the nursery is staffed by British nannies. Fortunately, the reality is far less stuffy than the image (though the stewards have not yet stooped to addressing us with 'Hi guys! What can I get you?') On the other hand, I am very suspicious of anyone who suggests that the service on *QM2* is anything less than impeccable. A few years ago a *New York Times* journalist wrote a piece about crossing the Atlantic on the *QM2,* but to my mind certain details don't ring true and I wonder whether he was even on board. For example, the journalist said that he tipped the maitre d' to get a good window table every evening, and alleged that one day his wife was propositioned in a bar by a good-looking waiter. I mean, does that kind of thing really go on? *Tipping* the maitre d'?

On the third evening, as is our custom, we skipped the Captain's Cocktail Party (on later crossings upgraded to Captain's Gala Reception). Mr Verne argued out of habit that free cocktails were a pretty good reason for putting on a suit an hour early, and that we'd be nicely warmed up for dinner conversation. I was having none of it – we'd never been to the Captain's Cocktail Party, the idea made me shudder, and I wasn't going to start now. Mr Verne thought it might be interesting to chat to the Captain, or if he was busy in the receiving line, to his officers; strangely, we are never invited to the Captain's table for dinner, and only ever would be if we were all three marooned on a desert island with nothing but coconuts to eat. I still wouldn't go, though.

We heard one elderly American comment approvingly that most gentlemen wore a tuxedo on formal nights, so it was fortunate he did not see Mr Verne in his plain old dark suit and tie. It's perfectly possible to complete a transatlantic crossing without once putting on formal clothes, though, and indeed for various reasons there will be passengers who cannot or do not want to dress up. We tried the experiment on a recent trip back from the US, when Mr Verne rebelled against having to dress up every evening. We therefore went to the Kings Court buffet-style restaurant for all our dinners and more or less spent the rest of the evening in our cabin, drinking wine and watching TV. We could also have gone to the lounge adjoining the Kings Court and to the Golden Lion pub, these being the only other areas where Cunard allows you to go casual on formal nights. The pub is just along from the formal Britannia restaurant, so plenty of scope there for the two extremes of fashion to co-exist briefly in passing. I suppose we did miss the fun of chatting to others (fun not guaranteed). I must admit that dinner in the Kings Court got to be a little tedious, the food often underwhelming and atmosphere non-existent. But, if you want to avoid all the formalities, you can.

The final evening was an anti-climax: no Baked Alaska at dinner! Yes, the old last-night tradition of dimming the restaurant lights for a parade of stewards bearing flaming Baked Alaskas seems to have been dropped. Sparklers had been a tame substitute for a few years but now… nothing. Never mind. We still loved the dear old *QM2*, and were sorry to be leaving her. A little sadly, we packed our cases and put them outside the cabin. It was the last night of this wonderful adventure around the world.

We disembarked in Southampton on a warm, bright day, retrieved our car from storage and headed north. Later that day the *QM2* was due to continue on to Hamburg with a large contingent of German passengers and, as we discovered during the week, a group of Mennonites from the Mid West, on their way to Germany and Switzerland to visit the lands of their forefathers.

During the drive home, we reflected on our nine-month odyssey. We had set off from these shores in late August, and not returned until June the following year. We had sailed on three cruise ships (one of them twice), and one cargo boat. We had crossed and re-crossed the Pacific Ocean, visiting Japan, South Korea, China, Vietnam, Singapore, Indonesia, Australia, and New Zealand, with the added bonus of seeing plenty of the USA and Canada along the way. We had spent 93 days on cruises, plus 199 days ashore in between. We had seen the world, got the most out of every minute good and bad, and never once set foot in an aircraft.

It can be done.

Around the World in 80 Cruise Ships: How We Cruise Hopped the Globe Without Ever Setting Foot in an Airport

What do you do if you want to travel the world but are too afraid to fly? You go by cruise ship, of course, hopping from one to another to get to your final destination and then home again. Sometimes you have to disembark in the middle of one cruise to catch the next – if the line and the port authorities will let you, that is. Sometimes you have to wait on land a while for the next cruise to turn up. You may be on a tiny ship with only a few hundred other passengers, or on a sleek leviathan for three thousand. You might like the ship, you might not (and this book tells it like it is). But you'll get there – without ever setting foot in an airport.

When the Vernes set off to see the Caribbean, Cuba, South America, the Falklands, Antarctica and the Panama Canal, they were determined never to fly (well, it was mostly cowardly Mrs Verne). They went there and back entirely by cruise ship, jumping from Cunard to Celebrity, from Holland America to P&O. In this frank and funny account they unpack the best and the worst about cruising and the many exotic locations they visited – and their dedicated resistance to the efforts of cruise lines to extort more money out of them.

https://www.amazon.com/Around-World-80-Cruise-Ships-ebook/dp/B07XP6XWXD

Printed in Great Britain
by Amazon

34186679R00149